Co-ordinated SCIENCE
Biology
Activities

Brian Beckett
Chris Goodwin

Oxford University Press

Oxford University Press, Walton Street, Oxford OX2 6DP
Oxford New York Toronto
Delhi Bombay Calcutta Madras Karachi
Petaling Jaya Singapore Hong Kong Tokyo
Nairobi Dar es Salaam Cape Town
Melbourne Auckland
and associated companies in
Berlin Ibadan

Oxford is a trade mark of Oxford University Press

ISBN 0 19 914312 9

Typeset by Microset Graphics, Basingstoke
Printed in Great Britain by
Scotprint Limited, Musselburgh
Produced by AMR for Oxford University Press

Contents

Getting started

The aim of this book is to help you learn the techniques and skills which biologists use to investigate the living world.

Techniques

You will learn basic techniques, including:

- how to use a microscope,
- how to use dissecting instruments,
- how to assemble apparatus for an experiment,
- how to handle apparatus safely,
- how to perform chemical tests on food and other materials,
- how to investigate living things in their natural environment.

Forming hypotheses and solving problems

Science is all about problem-solving. Why does this type of plant grow here and not over there? How do birds find their way across thousands of miles of land and sea during migrations? Does a new detergent harm the environment? Many exercises in this book give you the chance to solve problems by first guessing the answer. This is called **forming hypotheses,** and it involves looking for possible answers which fit all the known facts. In other words you think of the most likely explanation. Good hypotheses have the following features:

- they should not only explain known facts but allow you to predict that certain events are likely to occur,
- they should provide a **testable** explanation, which means that it must be possible to design an experiment to find out if the explanation is correct.

This book also includes many problem-solving exercises, usually under the heading **Find out.**

Designing experiments

Before you can solve a problem or test an hypothesis you must learn how to design controlled experiments.

Apparatus, materials and methods: Begin by listing the apparatus and materials you will need, then plan the experiment step by step, describing the procedures, tests and techniques you will use.

Controls: Imagine you are asked to find out if spraying a crop with pesticide will kill water weed in a nearby pond. You put water weed in a test tube, add pesticide and it dies. But would it have died in a test tube without pesticide? You need a **control** — another plant of identical weight and health, kept at the same temperature and with the same amount of light, and material nutrients etc., but without pesticide. In a controlled experiment *all* the conditions are kept the same *except* for the one being investigated.

Results tables: Design a results table *before* you start. You must decide what you are going to observe or measure and write appropriate headings for each column of the table.

Graphs: Decide which results must go along each axis. Choose a scale for each axis which is as large as the size of your graph paper will allow; label your axes and plot the points accurately. It is sometimes necessary to join points on a graph. If, when joining the points, the result is a zig zag line, you can draw a straight line or curve between the points so that there is roughly the same number of points on each side.

Interpreting results: You must extract information from tables and graphs and, if necessary, carry out simple calculations such as averages and percentages, in order to arrive at conclusions. Do your results tell you that your hypothesis is correct, or must you refine or re-think your hypothesis? Do they give you an answer to a problem and, of equal importance, do they suggest other problems to solve?

Evaluate your results: Criticize your work and think of ways it could be improved. Could it be improved by using different apparatus, materials, techniques or different ways of presenting results? Were the controls adequate?

Safety

It is very important that you:
- keep bags and coats well away from the work area where they won't cause accidents,
- leave hot tripods, glassware etc., to cool down before you touch them,
- leave Bunsens on a yellow flame when not in use so that the flame can be seen,
- wear goggles when strongly heating something,
- take care of expensive apparatus, or there will be nothing to do your practical with.

Main skills assessed:

The activities will help you to develop your experimental skills. They may also be used by your teacher to assess your ability to:

follow instructions
form hypotheses/solve problems
design and carry out experiments
use apparatus
make measurements
record and handle data
draw conclusions
criticize an experiment.

The main skills assessed are listed with each activity.

Microscopes

You need:

a microscope
prepared slides (e.g. insect head, wings, legs, etc.)

Main skills assessed:

Follow instructions
Use apparatus

The parts of a microscope

Coarse focus knob   This is used to get the specimen roughly in focus.

Fine focus knob   This is used to get the specimen in sharp focus.

Iris adjuster   This controls the amount of light reaching the specimen.

Light switch   For the bulb used to shine light through the specimen.

Eyepiece   This is the lens you look through.

Turret   This turns round so you can use different objective lenses.

Objective lenses   These have different powers of magnification. The longer the lens the greater its power to magnify specimens.

Stage   The platform that you put the specimen slides on. Slides are held down by a spring clip.

Using a microscope

1   Turn the turret until you have the low power objective lens (the short lens) in line with the eyepiece.

2   Clip a slide on the stage so that it is in the centre under the objective lens and look through the eyepiece.

3   Adjust the coarse focus until the specimen becomes clear. If necessary adjust the fine focus until the specimen is in sharp focus.

4   Move the iris adjuster until the specimen is clearly lit.

5   Calculate the magnification by multiplying the power of the eyepiece by the power of the objective lens (e.g. a × 5 eyepiece used with a × 15 objective magnifies 75 times).

6   Notice how, when you move the slide, the specimen seems to move in the opposite direction.

7   Change to the medium power objective. **Do not use the higher power objective yet**. Focus the microscope and notice that you now see much less of the specimen but at a higher magnification.

8   **How to use high power objectives**   If this is done carelessly the lens and a slide can be damaged.
    a) With your eyes level with the stage, slowly lower the high power objective until it *almost* touches the slide.
    b) Look through the eyepiece and focus by moving the lens *away from the slide* (i.e. always focus upwards). This avoids smashing the lens through a slide.

Making microscope slides

You need:

microscopes
mounted needles
slides and coverslips
scissors
pond or aquarium water
newspaper with words and pictures
crystals (salt, copper sulphate, sugar, potassium
    permanganate)
dropper pipettes

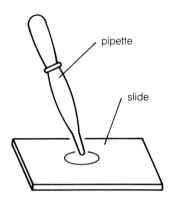

pipette

slide

Pond and aquarium water

Water from the bottom of a pond or aquarium, especially if it contains rotting vegetation, can contain many different protozoa and other microscopic creatures.

1 Use a bulb pipette to place one drop of pond or aquarium water onto the centre of a glass slide.

2 Place a coverslip with one edge resting on the slide near the drop of water. Use a mounted needle to lower it *slowly* onto the water. If you do this quickly you will trap air bubbles. Use just enough water to spread to the edges of the coverslip and no further. Place the slide on the microscope stage.

3 Start with low power magnification and search the slide for interesting objects, then change to medium or high power magnification.

4 Make notes and drawings of what you find.

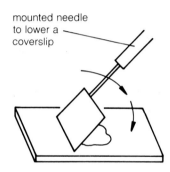

mounted needle
to lower a
coverslip

More things to do

5 Put a drop of tap water onto a slide. Remove a hair from your head, place it across the water and lower a coverslip over it. Study it under medium and high power magnification and make notes and drawings of the root end, the middle and the upper end of the hair.

6 Cut out pieces of newspaper small enough to fit under a coverslip. Mount them in water on slides. What is a newspaper photograph made up of?

7 Sprinkle some crystals on a *dry* slide. Study them without a coverslip. Prepare a table and use drawings and words to compare the shape and colour of four different types of crystal.

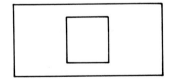

Correctly prepared slide

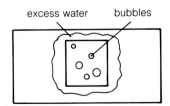

Badly prepared slide

excess water   bubbles

Looking at cells

A moss plant

leaf

You need:

microscopes	razors or scalpels
slides and coverslips	Petri dishes
forceps	onions
pig kidneys	moss plants

Moss leaf cells

1   Use forceps to take one leaf off a moss plant. Put the leaf on a slide, add a drop of water and lower a coverslip onto it.

2   Observe it under low, medium and high power. Identify as many parts as you can.

Onion cells

3   If you look at half an onion, you will see that it is made of fleshy leaves. Use a razor to cut a small piece out of one of the leaves. Use forceps to peel skin off the *inner* surface of the leaf. This skin is a thin layer of living cells. Put the skin into a Petri dish of water.

4   Put a drop of iodine stain onto a slide. Put a piece of onion skin into the stain and smooth it out so there are no folds. Lower a coverslip over it, taking care not to trap any bubbles. Prepare another slide in the same way but using water instead of iodine stain.

5   Study the stained onion cells under different magnifications, then look at unstained cells. What parts of the cells have become stained? How are onion cells *different from*, and *similar to* moss leaf cells?

Animal cells

6   Use a razor and forceps to peel small pieces of transparent skin off the outside of a kidney. Make a slide of the skin in water, and another in iodine.

7   Study stained and unstained cells. How are they different? Draw moss leaf, onion and animal cells and list their *similarities* and *differences*.

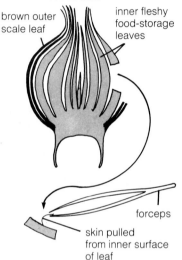

An onion cut in half

brown outer scale leaf

inner fleshy food-storage leaves

forceps

skin pulled from inner surface of leaf

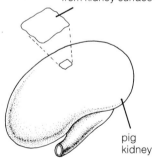

transparent skin from kidney surface

pig kidney

Main skills assessed:

Follow instructions
Use apparatus
Record and handle data

Measuring cells

Measuring a field of view

1 Place a clear plastic ruler under a microscope and focus on it with low power magnification. How many millimetres wide is the field of view?

2 **Problem**: Microscopic objects are measured in **micrometres** (one micrometre is written $1\mu m$). 1 mm = 1000 μm. Convert your field of view to micrometres.

Measuring onion cells

3 Prepare a slide of onion cells. Look at the slide under low power magnification. How many cells fit across the field of vision? In the drawing opposite, four and a half cells fill a field of view 2200 μm wide. What is the average length of each cell?

4 What is the average length, in micrometres, of onion cells in your slide? Turn the slide around and calculate the average width of the cells.

5 You now know the length in micrometres of one onion cell. Use this information, and your onion slide, to calculate the field of vision in micrometres under medium and high power magnification.

More things to do

6 Using the technique you have learned, measure:
   a) the length and width of moss leaf cells,
   b) the width of a human hair,
   c) the average size of sugar, salt and other crystals.

7 Look at permanent slides of insects and measure various parts, such as the width of scales on a butterfly's wing, the width of lenses in an insect's compound eye, the size of a fly's foot, etc.

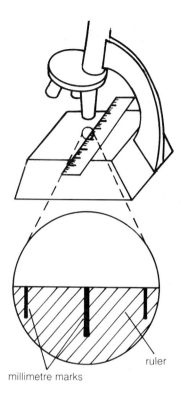

millimetre marks

ruler

The field of view is 2.2 mm.
What is this in micrometres?

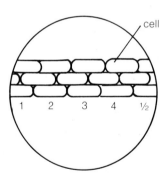

cell

The field of view is 2.2 mm.
What is the length of one cell,
in micrometres?

Diffusion

You need:	
500 cm³ and 50 cm³ beakers	red litmus paper
bent glass tubes	Indian ink
potassium permanganate	slides and coverslips
bell jar	microscopes
spatula	bulb pipettes

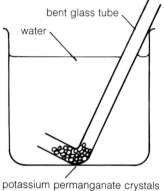

Method one

1 Pour water into a 500 cm³ beaker until it is three-quarters full.

2 Place some potassium permanganate crystals into the crook of a dry, bent glass tube.

3 Gently lower the tube into the beaker so that you disturb the crystals as little as possible.

4 Observe the apparatus over the next hour. Describe, and explain what you observe.

potassium permanganate crystals

Method two

5 Dip a piece of red litmus into ammonia solution and observe what happens.

6 Dampen some pieces of red litmus paper and use sticky tape to fasten them to the inside of a bell jar and the sides of a 50 cm³ beaker as shown in the diagram opposite.

7 Pour a little ammonia solution into the beaker, taking care not to splash any onto the litmus paper, and place the bell jar over the beaker.

8 Describe what happens to the litmus paper strips. In what order do they change colour? Explain what is happening.

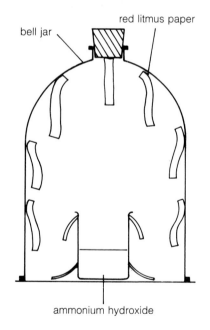

ammonium hydroxide

Find out: How fast do substances diffuse through air?

Design and carry out an experiment to find out how fast a scent, or other harmless strong smelling substance, diffuses through the air.

Start by thinking about the following:
How should you arrange pupils in the room before releasing the smell?
How are you going to time diffusion of the substance?
How are you going to present your results and conclusions?

Brownian motion and diffusion

1 Put a drop of water on a microscope slide then add one drop of Indian ink to it. Lower a cover slip over the liquid.

2 Put the slide onto a microscope stage and observe it under high power magnification.

3 Look very carefully at the particles of ink. What is happening to them? Can you explain what you see? If not, do some research.

4 This behaviour of tiny particles in water was first described by a scientist called Brown, which is why it is called **Brownian motion**.

5 How does Brownian motion help to explain what happens during diffusion?

Main skills assessed:

Follow instructions
Form hypotheses/solve problems
Design and carry out experiments
Use apparatus
Record and handle data
Criticize an experiment

Osmosis

You need:

microscopes	razor blades
slides and coverslips	bulb pipettes
slide labels	test tubes
potatoes	test tube racks
onions or rhubarb	white tiles
dandelion stems	scalpels
sugar	Petri dishes

Osmosis in potato cells

1 Make three potato cups from raw potatoes cut in half: cut a depression in the top, peel skin off the sides, and give each a flat base (see diagram opposite).

2 Boil one cup. Place the cups in Petri dishes of water. Pour sugar into the boiled cup and into one of the raw potato cups. Leave one cup empty.

3 Observe and describe what happens to the sugar, and what happens in the empty cup.
Explain what happens in the three cups.
Why was one cup left empty?
What conclusions can you draw about osmosis in living and dead cells?

Osmosis in dandelion stalks

4 Take two test tubes. Half-fill one with water and the other with strong sugar solution.

5 Obtain two dandelion stalks. Slit them upwards for about 2.5 cm, then make a second upward slit at right angles to the first to divide the stalk base into four strips (see diagram).

6 Put one stalk in water and the other in sugar solution and leave them for 10 minutes.

7 Observe and describe what happens.
What happens if you move the stalk in water to the sugar solution and vice versa?
Study the diagram opposite (or cut a thin slice of stalk and observe it under a microscope) and formulate a hypothesis to explain what you observed.

A – Empty potato cup

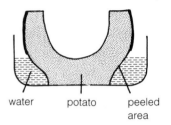

water   potato   peeled area

B – Raw potato cup with sugar

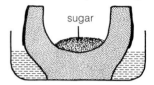

sugar

C – Boiled potato cup with sugar

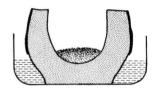

dandelion stalk

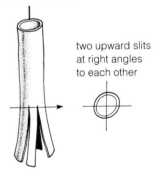

two upward slits at right angles to each other

Section through stalk

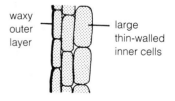

waxy outer layer   large thin-walled inner cells

Osmosis and plasmolysis

8 Either obtain strips of onion skin as described on page 8 or peel strips of coloured skin from rhubarb stalk (rhubarb is preferable for this experiment because its cells are filled with coloured pigment and this makes cell contents clearly visible).

9 Put drops of water onto one slide and strong sugar solution onto another. Label the slides so you know which is which.

10 Put onion or rhubarb skin into the liquid on each slide, lower a coverslip over it and observe the cells under high power magnification.

11 Describe and draw any changes which occur in cells in water and sugar solution.
Explain your observations.
What happens if the cells in sugar solution are washed and placed in water?

Find out: How do you find the osmotic pressure of cells?

Osmotic pressure is the pressure needed to stop water entering a solution by osmosis through a semi-permeable membrane. The stronger the solution the higher its osmotic pressure.

If you were given a range of different sugar solutions and told their osmotic pressures, how could you use them to find out the osmotic pressure of onion or rhubarb skin cells?
Design and carry out an experiment to do this.

Start by thinking about the following:
You have seen what happens to these cells in strong sugar solution. What would happen to them if placed in a solution with the *same* osmotic pressure as the cells?

How to prepare sugar solutions of known osmotic pressure

Dissolve 324 g of sugar in 500 cm³ of distilled water, then make it up to 1 litre. This gives a **molar** solution (1 gram-molecule per litre − written M/1).

The osmotic pressure of an M/1 sugar solution is 245 kPa. Divide the solution into five equal portions. Keep one portion at M/1 strength and dilute the others to obtain M/2, M/4, M/8 and M/16 solutions. Calculate the osmotic pressure of each.

Describe your method, results and conclusions.

> **Main skills assessed:**
>
> Follow instructions
> Form hypotheses/solve problems
> Design and carry out experiments
> Use apparatus
> Record and handle data
> Criticize an experiment

Variation

Main skills assessed:

Follow instructions
Use apparatus
Make measurements
Record and handle data
Draw conclusions
Criticize an experiment

1   Working in pairs, record the following information for both
    partners (refer to drawings below if necessary).
    a) Are your ears lobed or unlobed (drawing A)?
    b) Can you roll your tongue (drawing B)?
    c) What is the length of your little fingers, to
    the nearest millimetre (drawing C)?
    d) What is your weight, in kilograms?

2   Record your results
    a) Data for the whole class should be
    recorded in the form of a table on the
    blackboard (see opposite).
    b) Data should be used to draw histograms.
    A blank histogram for finger length is
    shown opposite.
    Draw others for the remaining data.

3   Use your results to decide which of the
    characteristics shows **continuous variation**
    and which shows **discontinuous variation**.

4   What other examples of variation can you
    think of? Try to think of an example using
    plants.

name	ear lobes yes/no	tongue rolling yes/no	finger length (mm)	weight (kg)

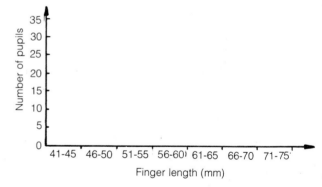

A Ears

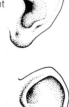

ear lobe present

ear lobe absent

B Tongue

rollers or non-rollers

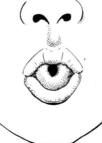

C Finger length (mm)

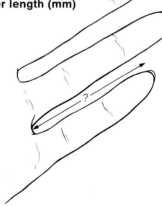

14

Genetics

H and h are alleles of the gene for hair colour. H is dominant and if it is present the hair is dark. If both alleles are h the hair is fair.

ova

		H	h
sperms	H	HH	Hh
	h	hH	hh

Look at the diagram above showing the zygotes which could be produced by a father with the genotype **Hh** and a mother with the genotype **Hh**. The diagram shows that zygotes with a **dominant allele (HH, Hh or hH)** are three times more likely to be produced than zygotes with two **recessive alleles (hh)**. In other words, dominant and recessive phenotypes occur in the ratio of 3:1.

This happens because:

- half the sperms carry the H allele and half carry the h allele,

- half the ova carry the H allele and half carry the h allele, and

- there is an equal chance that, during fertilization, any sperm can fertilize any ovum (i.e. fertilization is a **random process).**

This can be checked experimentally using coins to represent sperms and ova, and coin tossing to represent the random process of fertilization.

1 Work in groups of two. Each group should obtain two 2p coins. Use circular sticky labels to mark one side of one coin **sperm A** and the opposite side **sperm a**, then label one side of the other coin **ovum A** and the opposite side **ovum a**. Copy the chart below.

2 Working in pairs, spin the 'sperm coin' and the 'ovum coin' at the same time. Look at how they fall and enter the result in the appropriate part of the tally column. Repeat at least 50 times, then work out the totals.

3 Does the ratio of dominant to recessive phenotypes come to about 3:1?
Why must the coins be tossed at least 50 times to get reliable results?

4 What are the ratios if father's alleles are **aa** and mother's are **Aa**? Use this method to investigate inheritance of sex .

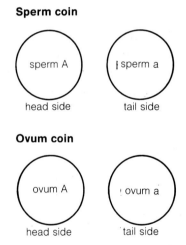

Sperm coin

sperm A — head side   sperm a — tail side

Ovum coin

ovum A — head side   ovum a — tail side

sperm	ovum	tally
A	A	
a	A	
A	a	
a	a	

total =

total =

Natural selection

There are two varieties of white clover: one with cyanide called **cyanose clover**, and another without cyanide called **acyanose clover**. There is a hypothesis that cyanide gives cyanose clover an advantage by discouraging herbivores such as slugs and snails. This could lead to natural selection in favour of cyanose plants. Test this hypothesis in the following way.

Identifying the types of clover

1 Find ten large clumps of white clover growing locally. Mark them with labels on sticks. Label ten specimen bottles 1 to 10. Place four leaves from clump 1 into bottle 1, four leaves from clump 2 into bottle 2, and so on.

2 Obtain freshly prepared sodium picrate paper. *Poisonous: handle only with forceps, and keep dry and away from light.*

3 Use a glass rod to crush a few drops of toluene and clover leaves together in a specimen tube. *Do not get toluene on the sides of the tube.*

4 *Quickly* suspend a picrate paper strip in the tube and seal it with a cork (see diagram). *The paper must not touch the toluene.* Repeat with the other tubes. After a day, cyanose clover will turn the picrate paper deep red or brown.

Testing for predator selection

5 Dig up small clumps of cyanose and acyanose clover with plenty of soil and undamaged roots. Set up two enamel dishes with equal-sized clumps of cyanose and acyanose clover in each. Label with label sticks. Note details such as the number and condition of leaves in each clump.

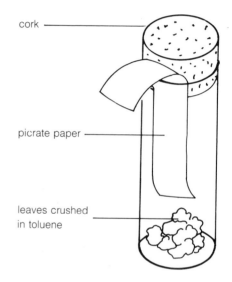

cork

picrate paper

leaves crushed in toluene

6 Put the two dishes in an aquarium, put 20 assorted slugs and snails among them and cover the aquarium with a glass sheet.

7 Each day record the number and condition of the leaves and the number of snails and slugs in each clump. Record your conclusions.

Find out:

If cyanide gives protection, why aren't all clover plants cyanose? It is known that cyanose clover is common at low altitudes and acyanose clover is common at high altitudes. One explanation **(hypothesis)** is that acyanose clover is less affected by the low (sometimes freezing) temperatures found at high altitudes than cyanose clover. Devise a controlled experiment to test this hypothesis.

Chlorophyll and photosynthesis

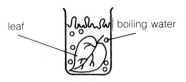

leaf · boiling water

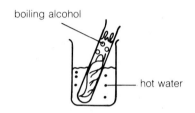

boiling alcohol · hot water

You need:

plants with normal and variegated leaves (tradescantia, coleus or geranium)	forceps
	500 cm³ beakers
	white tiles
iodine solution	Bunsen burners
boiling tubes	tripods and gauzes
	ethanol (alcohol)

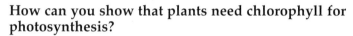

How can you show that plants need chlorophyll for photosynthesis?

You need a way of showing that photosynthesis has taken place. Plants change sugar produced by photosynthesis into starch and store it in their leaves. So a leaf with starch has been carrying out photosynthesis.

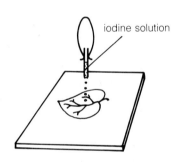

iodine solution

Testing a leaf for starch

1 Take a leaf from a non-variegated plant which has been in the light for a few hours. *SAFETY: put goggles on*. Half fill a 500 cm³ beaker with water and bring it to the boil. Put the leaf in the water for about 30 seconds then *turn the Bunsen off*.

2 Half fill a boiling tube with ethanol. *SAFETY: this is highly inflammable so do not put it near a naked flame*. Use forceps to take the boiled leaf out of the water and transfer it to the ethanol. Put the tube of ethanol into the beaker of very hot water. The ethanol will boil and remove chlorophyll from the leaf, making test results easier to see.

3 Lift the leaf out of the ethanol, dip it into the hot water to soften it, spread it out on a white tile and cover it with iodine solution. A blue-black colour indicates the presence of starch in the leaf.

A variegated tradescantia leaf

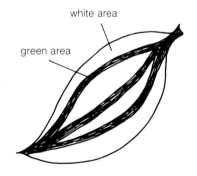

white area

green area

Find out:

You are provided with **variegated** leaves − leaves which have areas with, and without chlorophyll. How can you use these and the test above to show that chlorophyll is necessary for photosynthesis? Record results by drawing a leaf before and after testing.

Main skills assessed:

Follow instructions
Form hypotheses/solve problems
Design and carry out experiments
Criticize an experiment

Light, carbon dioxide and photosynthesis

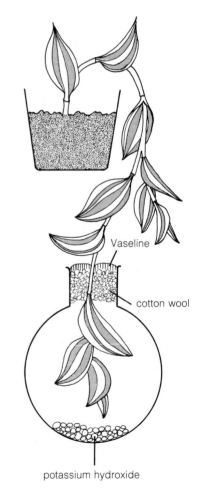

You need:

potted plants	iodine solution
scissors	paper clips
ethanol	potassium hydroxide
white tiles	conical flasks
boiling tubes	clamps and stands
500 cm³ beakers	cotton wool
Bunsens, tripods and gauzes	Vaseline
black paper or polythene	spatulas

Main skills assessed:

Follow instructions
Form hypotheses/solve problems
Design and carry out experiments
Criticize an experiment

Do plants need light for photosynthesis?

1   You could test two plants for starch − one which had been in the dark for 12 hours and one which had been in the light. But perhaps you can think of more interesting experiments using the materials provided?

2   How could you use strips of black paper or polythene, or even a black and white 35 mm photographic negative?

3   At which stage will you detach the experimental leaf from the plant?

4   Predict what a leaf will look like after the starch test. Make drawings of your results.

Find out: Do plants need carbon dioxide for photosynthesis?

You could use the apparatus in the drawing opposite.
Why must you start with a plant which has been in the dark for 12 hours?
Why must you test a leaf for starch *before* setting up the apparatus opposite?
Find out what the potassium hydroxide will do to air in the flask.
SAFETY: take care, it could burn your skin or the leaves, and is very poisonous.
Why is the Vaseline necessary?
What control is needed?
Where will you put the plant and for how long?
What test is needed to obtain a result?
How will you present results and conclusions?

Vaseline

cotton wool

potassium hydroxide

Photosynthesis and oxygen

You need:

a litre beaker	Bunsen burner
glass funnel	bench lamp
test tube	sodium hydrogencarbonate
Plasticine	spatula
wood splint	pond weed (*Elodea*)

1   Three-quarters fill a 1 litre beaker with water in which a small amount of sodium hydrogencarbonate has been dissolved. This will supply the plants with carbon dioxide.

2   Put a few springs of healthy pond weed such as *Elodea* in the bottom of the beaker. Place a glass funnel over the pond weed. Use one or more lumps of Plasticine to raise the rim of the funnel off the base of the beaker, so the liquid can circulate freely. Make sure the liquid level is well above the end of the funnel.

3   Fill a test tube with weak sodium hydrogencarbonate solution. Put your thumb over the end, turn the tube upside down and lower it into the beaker without letting in any air. When the end of the test tube is under the liquid remove your thumb and lower the tube onto the funnel, as shown in the diagram.

4   Either put the apparatus on a well-lit window ledge or place it near a bench lamp.

5   After about a week sufficient gas should have collected in the tube to test.

Lift the test tube off the funnel but do not let in any air. Put your thumb over the end of the tube, lift it out of the beaker and turn it right way up. Do not remove your thumb yet.

Test the gas for the presence of oxygen: light a wood splint and when it is burning brightly blow it out so the end is glowing red hot. Lift your thumb off the test tube and *very quickly* lower the glowing wood splint into it. Observe closely what happens.

6   **Questions:**
Does the tube contain pure oxygen?
Can you devise a control for this experiment?

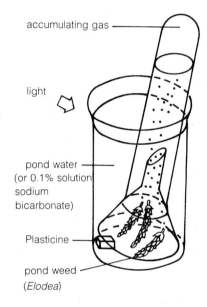

accumulating gas

light

pond water (or 0.1% solution sodium bicarbonate)

Plasticine

pond weed (*Elodea*)

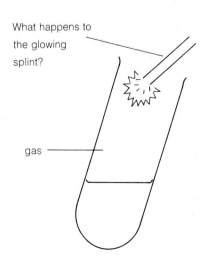

What happens to the glowing splint?

gas

Photosynthesis: problems to solve

You need:	
test tubes and racks	Plasticine
pond weed (*Elodea*)	balances
bench lamps	rulers
sodium hydrogencarbonate	spatulas

Main skills assessed:

Follow instructions
Form hypotheses/solve problems
Design and carry out experiments
Criticize an experiment

Find out: Does light intensity affect photosynthesis?

A simple way of measuring the rate of photosynthesis is to count the bubbles of gas produced by a pond weed such as *Elodea* (see drawing opposite).

Start by thinking about the following:

How are you going to achieve different light intensities? If you halve the distance between a plant and a light source, light intensity increases four times. How is this information useful?

Decide if you are going to place several plant samples at different light intensities or use only one plant sample. If you use several what points must you note when choosing them?

How can you keep all other conditions the same while you vary light intensity?

Is there a point at which further increase in light intensity produces no further increase in photosynthesis? If so what factor could be preventing further increase?

Find out: Does temperature affect photosynthesis?

Use the same apparatus as above.
What range of temperatures are you going to investigate, and how are you going to achieve these temperatures?
How will you keep all other conditions the same while you vary temperature?
Could the experiment above help you decide on a standard light intensity?
Is there a best (**optimum**) temperature for photosynthesis at this light intensity?

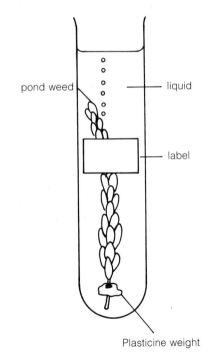

pond weed — liquid

label

Plasticine weight

Plant senses

Geotropism

1 A **clinostat** is used to rotate plants slowly in any plane (see diagram A).

2 Germinate bean seeds until they have straight roots about 1 cm long. Pin one seedling, and a pad of damp cotton wool, onto the clinostat and replace the cylinder, as shown in diagram A.

3 Pin another seedling and damp cotton wool, to a piece of cork and cover it with a beaker or glass jar (diagram B).

4 Start the clinostat rotating and put both pieces of apparatus in the dark for three or four days.

5 **Questions:**
Which apparatus is the control?
What is the damp cotton wool for?
What happens to the two seedlings?
Why was the apparatus put in the dark?
Explain why rotation in a clinostat has this effect.

A

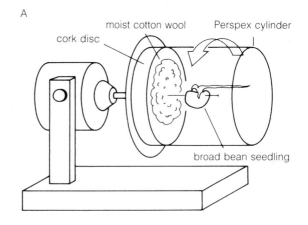

B

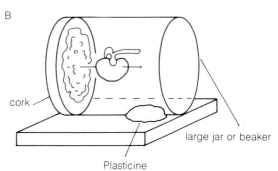

Find out: How to use a clinostat to investigate phototropism

Sprinkle a few cress seeds onto damp filter paper in the bottom of two Petri dishes. Design an experiment, using the clinostat, to show the effects on growth of light from one direction.

Start by thinking about the following:
What part could a clinostat play?
How will you arrange for light to come from only one direction?
Predict your results before you start.

Germination and growth

You need:

cress and pea seeds   cotton wool

paper towels   test tubes and racks

500 cm³ beakers   paraffin oil

balances   refrigerator

Germination

1   Label five test tubes 1 to 5.

2   Put cress seeds in tube 1 and place it in a warm, well-lit place. These seeds have warmth, air and light but no water.

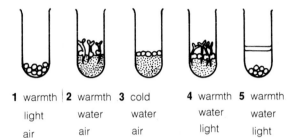

1 warmth	**2** warmth	**3** cold	**4** warmth	**5** warmth
light	water	water	water	water
air	air	air	light	light
			air	

3   Put cress seeds on wet cotton wool in tube 2 and place it in a warm dark place. These seeds have warmth, air and water but no light.

4   Put cress seeds on wet cotton wool in tube 3 and place it in a refrigerator. These seeds have water and air but no warmth or light.

5   Put cress seeds on wet cotton wool in tube 4 and place it in a warm, well-lit place. These seeds have warmth, water, air and light.

6   Put cress seeds in tube 5 and cover them with boiled and cooled water (boiling drives oxygen out of the water), then pour a little paraffin oil onto the water to keep oxygen out. Place the tube in a warm, well-lit place. These seeds have warmth, water and light but no oxygen.

7   Examine the tubes after about three days. In which tubes have seeds germinated? What conditions are necessary for seeds to germinate?

Growth curves

If you weigh organisms as they grow and plot your results on a graph the result is a curved shape called a **growth curve**. Plot two different growth curves as follows.

8   Soak 40 peas in water for 12 hours then wrap them in wet paper towelling. Put the wrapped peas in beakers of water in a warm, dark place (see diagram opposite).

9   Every three days remove five seedlings and find their average weight. Then heat them at 100°C until they are completely dry and find their average weight again. Plot graphs for wet and dry weight changes.

10   Explain why the wet and dry growth curves are different. What conclusions can you draw about the early growth of plants from these results?

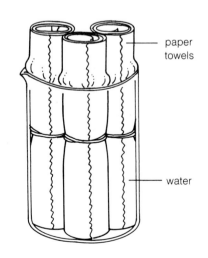

paper towels

water

Transport tissue in plants

Water-conducting tissue of celery

1   Obtain a stick of celery, preferably with leaves still attached. Put it in a beaker half-filled with eosin dye and leave it for 24 hours.

2   Look carefully at the leaf veins. Observe and describe what has happened. Explain what has happened.

3   Lay the celery on a white tile and use a razor to cut thin slices off it. Continue until you have a slice so thin it is almost transparent.

4   Use a paint brush to transfer the slice to a microscope slide, add a drop of water and lower a coverslip over it.

5   Make a drawing of the slide showing which areas have turned red. What are these areas? Refer to page 46 of the text book.

Compare root and stem of beans

6   Germinate a number of broad bean seeds by trapping them against the sides of a jam jar with a cylinder of blotting paper filled with damp sand or saw dust. Leave them until the root and stem have developed.

7   Clamp a bean over a beaker of eosin so that its root is immersed in the dye. Leave it until the dye becomes visible in the leaf veins.

8   Cut thin slices of the root and stem, and make drawings to show which areas have been stained red.
What is the difference between the position of xylem in a bean stem and root?

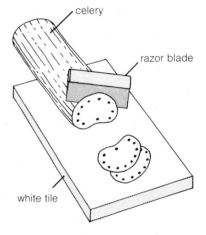

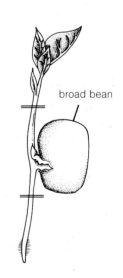

broad bean

Transparation

Main skills assessed:

Follow instructions
Form hypotheses/solve problems
Design and carry out experiments
Use apparatus
Make measurements
Record and handle data
Draw conclusions
Criticize an experiment

You need:

bell jar	sheet of glass
plant in pot (e.g. geranium)	Vaseline
polythene bag	privet or lilac leaves

Transpiration in a potted plant

1 Water a potted plant and let all excess water drain away. Put the pot inside a polythene bag and tie it firmly so that water cannot evaporate from the soil. Weigh the plant in its sealed pot.

2 Put Vaseline around the bottom edge of a bell jar. Put the plant onto a glass plate and place the bell jar over it so it is sealed from outside air (see diagram opposite). Leave the apparatus for a week.

3 Observe and describe any changes in the bell jar. Take the plant out and weigh it. Note any change.
If the plant has lost weight where and how could this have happened?
Does this experiment *prove* that plants lose water (**transpire**) through their leaves?
If not, exactly what *does* it prove, or demonstrate?

Find out: Through which surface do leaves lose water?

The experiment above suggests that plants lose water through their leaves during transpiration. But through which surface does the water evaporate? Design and carry out an experiment to find out.

Start by thinking about the following:
Privet and lilac leaves are plentiful and easy to handle.
Vaseline can be used to put a waterproof coat on a leaf to prevent evaporation.
How many leaves will you need and what should you look for when choosing them?
Label the leaves with sticky labels and decide where each leaf must be coated with Vaseline.
What else must be recorded before the leaves are left to dry?
Don't forget a control.
After a week record your results and conclusions.
Criticize your method and suggest improvements.

bell jar

plant

glass sheet

plastic bag

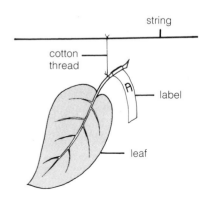

string

cotton thread

label

leaf

Stomata

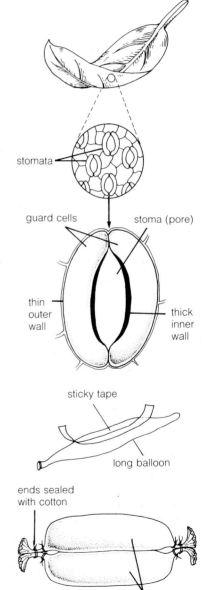

Looking at stomata

1 It is possible to tear a privet leaf so that a small area of lower skin is exposed. Hold a leaf with its lower surface uppermost and tear it diagonally rather than straight across.

2 Make a microscope slide of lower skin and look at it under a magnification of at least × 600.

3 Estimate the size, in micrometres, of stomata (see page 9). Roughly how many stomata are there per square millimetre of leaf surface?

A balloon model of a guard cell

4 Fasten a length of sticky tape to one side of a long balloon. Inflate the balloon and compare its shape with another balloon without the sticky tape.

Problem: Guard cells have thicker walls next to the stoma than on their outer walls (diagram above). Think about the shape of the balloon with the sticky tape, and formulate an hypothesis to explain the function of a guard cell's thick inner wall. What effect could it have as guard cells inflate and deflate to open and close a stoma?

More things to do

Make a visking tube model of stomata.
Fill two 20 cm lengths of visking tube with strong sugar solution and seal both ends with cotton. Tie the two visking sausages firmly together, place them in water for 30 minutes and explain what happens.
What do the two visking sausages represent?
Use this result to formulate an hypothesis to explain how stomata open and close.

stomata

guard cells   stoma (pore)

thin outer wall   thick inner wall

sticky tape

long balloon

ends sealed with cotton

visking tube filled with strong sugar solution

Measuring transpiration

You need:

privet or other leafy twigs	cotton wool
capillary tubes	rubber tubing
Vaseline	labelled specimen tubes

Making a potometer

1   Set up the apparatus opposite in the following way.
    Push the piece of rubber tubing about 2 cm over the end of the
    capillary tube, submerge in water and squeeze the rubber tube
    until *both* tubes are full.
    Push the end of the twig into the rubber tube (don't wet the
    leaves) and, without letting water escape, clamp the apparatus
    over a beaker of water. Seal all joints with Vaseline and fasten
    a card scale in position (see diagram).

2   After five minutes raise the apparatus so the capillary is out of
    the water. Air should start to move up the capillary. How far
    does it move in two minutes? Find the average time for three
    two-minute runs.

3   What *exactly* have you measured?
    Is what you measured the same as transpiration?
    How could you measure the *volume* of water the twig takes up
    each minute?

Find out: The effects of climate on transpiration

Method one

Devise an experiment using the apparatus above to discover the
effects on the twig of five *different* climatic conditions (listed in
method two).

Method two

What *measurable* change will take place in the apparatus opposite
with time?
What will cause this change?

Design an experiment using this apparatus to discover the effects
on transpiration of hot, cold, windy, humid and dark conditions.

Start by thinking about the following:
How you will create these conditions?
What will you measure, and when?
What controls are needed and how will you record your results?
Remember, when one condition is changed the others must
remain the same.

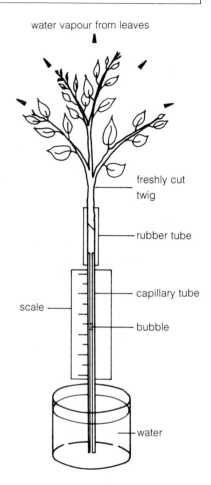

water vapour from leaves

freshly cut twig

rubber tube

scale

capillary tube

bubble

water

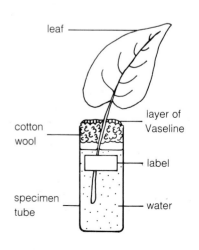

leaf

cotton wool

layer of Vaseline

label

specimen tube

water

Bones

<table>
<tr><td colspan="2">You need:</td></tr>
<tr><td>glass rods
   (hollow and solid)</td><td>retort stands
clamps</td></tr>
<tr><td>metre rules</td><td>chicken leg bones</td></tr>
<tr><td>Bunsen burner</td><td>weak hydrochloric acid</td></tr>
<tr><td>tongs</td><td>hook weights</td></tr>
</table>

Main skills assessed:

Follow instructions
Use apparatus
Record and handle data
Draw conclusions
Criticize an experiment

Investigating bone structure

Bone contains **minerals** (mainly calcium compounds) and **organic fibres**. What is the function of these parts?

1   Obtain two small bones (e.g. chicken leg bones). Remove the minerals from one bone by soaking it in dilute hydrochloric acid for 24 hours. Soak another bone in water for the same time (the control).

2   Pour away the acid, wash the bone and try to bend it. Compare it with the bone soaked in water. What do your observations tell you about the functions of minerals and organic fibres in bones?

3   Remove the organic fibres from another small bone by holding it (with tongs) in a hot Bunsen flame for a few minutes in a fume cupboard.

4   When it is cool, try to crush the burnt end with a pencil or stick. What do your observations tell you about the functions or organic fibres in bones?

Why are bones hollow?

Bones are not solid. They consist of an outer cylinder of hard (**compact**) bone which surrounds a central **marrow cavity**. Is there any advantage to this arrangement? Try to find out, as follows.

5   Obtain a solid and a hollow glass rod, each about 30 cm long. Clamp them so they are supported horizontally about a metre above a bench.

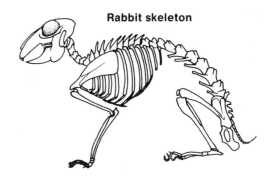

Rabbit skeleton

6   *SAFETY: put on goggles.* Attach weights to the centre of each rod until they break. Record your results and see if they give you a reason why bones are hollow. Suggest other reasons.

Why are backbones arched?

Look at the skeleton of a rabbit or other four-legged animal and note the shape of its backbone. Is there an advantage in having an arched backbone?

7   Support a metre rule (or strip of wood) on chair backs or clamp stands so that each end overlaps the support by 1 cm. Attach weights to its centre until it bends and falls off the supports.

8   Place a metre rule between two supports in such a way that when the supports are moved towards each other the rule arches upwards slightly.

9   Attach weights to its centre as before. What do your results tell you about the advantage of having an arched backbone?

Muscle fatigue

Main skills assessed:

Follow instructions
Record and handle data
Draw conclusions
Criticize an experiment

A test of strength

1   Work in pairs. One member makes accurate timings, in seconds, while the other performs a task.

2   One member must hold a book or other heavy object in his/her preferred hand (i.e. right hand if right-handed) so that it is at arm's length. The arm must be straight out at the shoulder and must be kept in this position for as long as possible.

3   The time-keeper starts timing as soon as the book is in the required position and stops when the book is lowered or the arm bent. Record how long the weight is held.

4   The pair now swap tasks and repeat this procedure.
The pair swap tasks again but this time the book is held in the *non-preferred hand*.
The pair swap tasks again so that the other member tries the task with his/her non-preferred hand.

5   Results for each pupil should be recorded on the blackboard then converted into a table showing how many pupils held the weight, in each hand, for intervals such as 60-69 seconds, 70-79 seconds etc. up to the longest time recorded.

6   Convert these results into histograms for preferred and non-preferred hands.
Explain any differences between preferred and non-preferred hands.
Explain any differences between the sexes.
What caused fatigue in muscles?

Investigating muscle fatigue

7   Use the results of the previous experiment to find four pupils who are roughly equal in strength.

8   **Pupil one** holds a weight at arm's length, as described in the previous experiment, for as long as possible. He/she rests for 10 seconds and then repeats the task.
Continue in this way for five repetitions or until the pupil is too tired to go on.
Record, in seconds, the time the weight is held for each repetition.

9   **Pupil two** does the same as pupil one except that a rest of 20 seconds is allowed between repetitions.

10   **Pupil three** does the same as pupil one except that a rest of 30 seconds is allowed between repetitions.

11 · **Pupil four** does the same as pupil one except that a rest of 40 seconds is allowed between repetitions.

12   Construct a table showing how long each pupil held the weight held during each repetition.

13   **Questions:**
What effect on performance did the different rest periods have?
Try to explain these differences (relate them to the efficiency of the circulatory system, anaerobic respiration and the oxygen debt).

Anaerobic respiration

Main skills assessed:

Follow instructions
Use apparatus
Record and handle data
Draw conclusions
Criticize an experiment

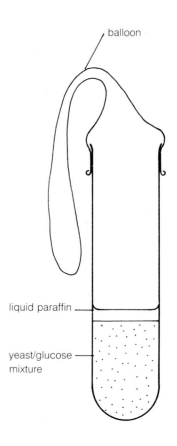

balloon

liquid paraffin

yeast/glucose mixture

Anaerobic respiration (fermentation) in yeast

1. Label three test tubes A, B and C.
   Place 20 cm³ of yeast suspended in cold, boiled water into tube A. (Boiling removes oxygen from water.) Add a few drops of liquid paraffin (enough to cover the surface of the yeast suspension).
   Place 20 cm³ of glucose dissolved in cold, boiled water into tube B. Add liquid paraffin.
   Place 10 cm³ of yeast suspended in cold, boiled water into tube C, then add 10 cm³ of glucose dissolved in cold, boiled water. Mix the two together. Add a few drops of liquid paraffin.

2. Place a balloon firmly over the neck of each tube (tie with cotton if necessary). Make sure the balloon is deflated. Put the tubes in a warm place for 24 hours.

3. Record what happens to the balloons.
   Explain your observations.
   Why was cold, boiled water used in this experiment?
   Why was liquid paraffin added to each tube?
   What gas entered a balloon?

Anaerobic respiration in peas

4. Fit two Thermos flasks with bungs through which a thermometer has been passed. Label the flasks A and B.

5. Fill flask A with boiled peas in cold, boiled water containing bactericide.
   Fill flask B with fresh peas in cold, boiled water.
   Note the temperature of each flask.

6. Place the bung in each flask, so that air cannot enter and leave them for a week. Note any temperature changes daily.

7. Explain any changes which occur in the temperature, and in the peas.
   Why was one set of peas boiled?
   Why were both sets of peas in boiled, cold water?
   Why was bactericide added to flask A?

Lung volume

You need:

bell jar with 500 cm³   rubber tube
   graduations down one side   deep sink
50% alcohol

Main skills assessed:

Follow instructions
Use apparatus
Record and handle data
Criticize an experiment

Breathe in as much air as you can, then breathe out as much air as you can. The volume of air which you breathed out is called the **vital capacity** of your lungs.

After you have forced as much air as possible out of your lungs there is still about 1500 cm³ left behind. This is called the **residual volume** of your lungs.

The **total volume** of your lungs is your vital capacity *plus* your residual volume.

1 Mark out the side of a bell jar in 500 cm³ units as follows:
   Place a bung firmly in a bell jar and turn it upside down in a sink (bung downwards). Pour 500 cm³ of water into the bell jar and mark the water level with a chinagraph pencil or indelible marker.
   Repeat until the whole of one side is marked out.

2 Fill a deep sink with water.
   Place the bell jar on its side in the water so that it is completely full.
   Without letting in any air, turn the bell jar upright in the sink. Run water out of the sink until it is about half full.

3 Work in pairs.
   One pupil tilts the bell jar enough to let in a rubber tube (see diagram) and then holds the tube in place.
   The other pupil breathes in as much air as possible and then blows out as much air as possible through the rubber tube into the bell jar.

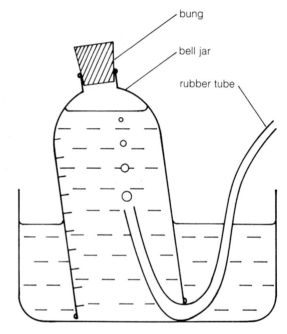

bung

bell jar

rubber tube

Raise the bell jar so that the level of water inside is level with water in the sink, and read off and record the vital capacity of your lungs.
Sterilize the end of the rubber tube in alcohol then wash it in water.
Swap tasks and repeat this procedure.
Prepare a class results table on the blackboard.

4 What is the total volume of your lungs?
   What is the average vital capacity of your class?
   What is the smallest and the largest vital capacity in your class?

Breathing and gas exchange

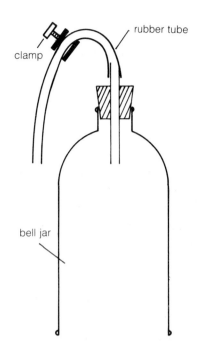

You need:

bell jar with 500 cm³ graduations down one side	rubber bung with glass tube through it
deep sink	rubber tube with clamp
wood splints	candle in saucer

1   Prepare a bell jar with 500 cm³ graduations as described in the last experiment. Fit it with a rubber bung, rubber tube and clamp (see diagram). Close the rubber tube by tightening the clamp.

2   Float a saucer with a lighted candle on it in a sink half-filled with water. Place a bell jar over the lighted candle.

3   Note the size of the candle flame and how long it burns. When the candle has gone out raise the bell jar so that the level of water inside is level with water in the sink. Read off the volume of air in the bell jar. Lift the bell jar and candle out of the water.

4   Place the bell jar on its side in the sink, and pour enough water into the sink so that the bell jar is full
Without letting in any air turn the bell jar upright in the sink.

5   Take a deep breath and hold it as long as possible. Open the clamp on the rubber tube and blow air through it into the bell jar. Place your thumb over the end of the tube so that air does not escape while you take another breath and hold it as long as possible. Blow this into the bell jar. Repeat until the bell jar is full of breathed air then close the rubber tube by tightening the clamp.

6   Refloat the lighted candle on the water. Raise one edge of the bell jar just enough to let you introduce the candle. Do this so that *as little fresh air as possible gets into the bell jar.*

7   Note the size of the candle flame and how long it burns. When the candle has gone out raise the bell jar so the level of water inside is level with water in the sink. Read off the volume of air in the bell jar.

8   **Questions:**
Oxygen supports combustion. What does this experiment tell you about the amount of oxygen in laboratory air and breathed air? How is combustion similar to respiration? Suggest improvements to this experiment then re-design it to obtain more accurate results.

Main skills assessed:

Follow instructions
Use apparatus
Record and handle data
Criticize an experiment

Demonstrating respiration

You need:

boiling tube and rubber
  bung with two holes
limewater
glass tubing

four conical flasks and four
  rubber bungs with two
  holes each
rubber tubing

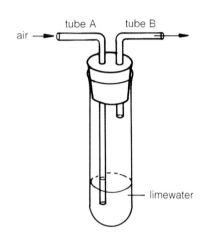

Compare breathed and unbreathed air

1 Prepare the apparatus opposite. How long
does it take for limewater to turn milky when
you blow air gently down tube A?
Wash out the boiling tube and refill with
fresh limewater. How long does it take for
limewater to turn milky when you suck air
gently through tube B?

2 **Questions:**
What turns limewater milky?
What do your results tell you about the
difference between laboratory air and
breathed air?
What exactly do your results prove?

Demonstrate respiration in animals and plants

3 Set up the apparatus below.
What is the purpose of flask 1?
Why is flask 2 necessary?
What does the apparatus demonstrate?

4 Investigate wood-lice, maggots, earthworms
etc., in a small specimen chamber. Use a bell
jar to investigate bigger animals.

5 **Problem:** How could you use this
apparatus to make rough comparisons of
respiration rate in, for example, woodlice and
earthworms?
What things would you have to keep the
same?
How would you set up the apparatus to
demonstrate respiration in plants?

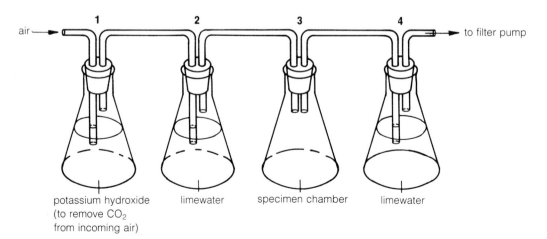

Measuring respiration

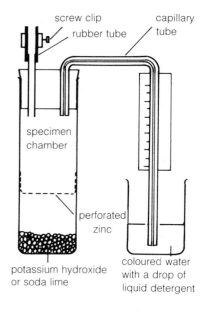

screw clip   capillary tube
rubber tube
specimen chamber
perforated zinc
potassium hydroxide or soda lime
coloured water with a drop of liquid detergent

You need:

specimen tubes and bungs with two holes
potassium hydroxide
50 cm³ beakers
capillary tubing

perforated zinc
ink (coloured water)
white card
sticky tape

1   Prepare the apparatus opposite. It is a simple **respirometer**; that is, it can be used to measure the rate of respiration. Predict what will happen to coloured liquid in the capillary tube if you put a few maggots or other small creatures in the specimen chamber and closed the screw clip.
What is the reasoning behind your prediction?

2   Carry out this experiment and check your prediction. Aerobic organisms take in oxygen and produce carbon dioxide at about the same rate. Carbon dioxide is absorbed by the potassium hydroxide (or soda lime). Use these facts to explain your result.

Find out: How to measure respiration rate in a variety of small animals

What exactly does this apparatus measure?

Design an experiment to measure and compare respiration rate in small creatures such as woodlice, beetles, spiders, earthworms, maggots etc.

Start by thinking about the following:
What conditions must be kept the same for each creature so that results can be compared?
How could you improve your results if you knew the diameter (bore) of the capillary tube?
Why is the rubber tube and screw clip essential, and when should the clip be opened and closed?

Find out: How temperature affects respiration rate

Design an experiment to measure the respiration rate of, for example maggots, at a range of temperatures from 0 °C to 40 °C.

Start by thinking about the following:
How are you going to maintain a constant temperature in the specimen chamber?
When should the screw clip be opened and closed?
Is one measurement at each temperature enough? If not, then why are more temperature measurements needed?

Main skills assessed:

Follow instructions
Form hypotheses/solve problems
Design and carry out experiments
Use apparatus
Record and handle data
Criticize an experiment

Pulse and breathing rates

> **You need:**
>
> clocks or watches with second hands
> bench or chair about 30 cm high

Investigate the effects of exercise on pulse and breathing rates

1 Form groups of three.

2 One member performs a series of tasks described in **4** below. Another measures the first person's pulse rate, and another measures the first person's breathing rate.

   Pulse rate: Use the method shown in the diagram. *Immediately* a task has been completed, measure the pulse for 30 seconds and multiply the result by 2 to get the pulse rate per minute.

   Breathing rate: *Immediately* after a task has been completed count the number of breaths in 30 seconds and multiply by 2 to get the breathing rate per minute.

3 Swap jobs until all have performed each task.

4 Record breathing and pulse rates after each member of the group has:
   * sat at rest for two minutes,
   * walked on the spot for one minute,
   * jogged on the spot for one minute,
   * run as fast as possible on the spot for up to one minute.
   Record the class's results.

5 **Questions:**
   What were the highest, lowest and average breathing rates for each task?
   What were the highest, lowest and average pulse rates for each task?
   Draw a graph to show how your pulse and breathing rate changed with exercise.
   Draw a graph to show how the **class average** pulse and breathing rates changed with exercise.
   How do *your* results compare with the class average?
   Why do breathing and pulse rates change in this way with exercise?

A standardized fitness test

6 Work in pairs. One member performs the following task while the other calls out at minute intervals, and then measures the first member's pulse rate.

7 Face a bench about 30 cm high. Step onto it with one foot then step up with the other foot. Step down with the first foot then step down with the second foot.
Repeat this sequence 25 times a minute for three minutes (practise first to get the speed right).

8 *Immediately* afterwards measure and record your pulse rate for 30 seconds. Multiply by 2 to get your pulse rate per minute. Record how long it takes for your pulse to return to resting rate.

9 **Questions:**
What are the fastest, slowest and average pulse rates for the class?
What are the fastest, slowest and average times in which pulse rates return to normal for the class?
Compare your result with these.
Is the fittest person the one with the slowest or fastest pulse rate? Explain your answer.
Is the fittest person the one whose pulse took the shortest or the longest time to return to normal? Explain your answer.

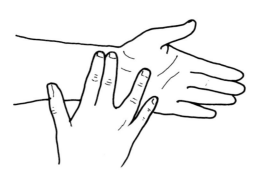

Main skills assessed:

Follow instructions
Use apparatus
Make measurements
Record and handle data
Draw conclusions
Criticize an experiment

Temperature homeostasis

You need:

strips of cobalt chloride paper in a desiccator

sticking plasters

clinical thermometers

1 Work in pairs. One member carries out a task while the other makes observations. Swap tasks and repeat.

2 Take a strip of dry cobalt chloride paper and moisten it with a drop of water. What happens to its colour?
Note this colour change because you will have to look for it in this experiment.

3 Use sticking plaster to attach dry cobalt chloride paper to the forehead of one member, so that most of the paper is visible. Observe any colour change while the subject sits quietly. If nothing has happened after five minutes record the result as '5 minutes +'. Measure the subject's skin temperature under an armpit.
Remove the cobalt chloride paper.

4 The subject should walk on the spot for two minutes. Immediately afterwards attach a fresh strip of cobalt chloride paper to the subject's forehead, record how long it takes to change colour then remove it.
At the same time record the subject's skin temperature, as above.

5 The subject should jog on the spot for two minutes. Immediately afterwards attach a fresh strip of cobalt chloride paper to the subject's forehead, record how long it takes to change colour then remove it.
At the same time record the subject's skin temperature, as above.

6 The subject should run hard on the spot for at least one minute. Immediately afterwards attach a fresh strip of cobalt chloride paper to the subject's forehead, record how long it takes to change colour then remove it.
At the same time record the subject's skin temperature, as before.

7 **Questions:**
What does the cobalt chloride paper test tell you about changes in the skin during exercise?
What do skin temperature measurements tell you about changes in the skin during exercise?
Explain why these changes occurred.
What results might have been obtained if body temperature (e.g. from the mouth) rather than skin temperature had been measured?

More things to do

Design an experiment to study the relationship between exercise and perspiration while wearing different amounts of clothing.

Design an experiment to study the relationship between exercise and perspiration in different environmental conditions.

List different environmental conditions and work out how you can create them.
What other conditions must remain the same?

The functions of perspiration

You need:

thermometers   cotton wool
small beakers of water
    and alcohol

1   Wave your hand backwards and forwards in front of you. Does it feel warmer or cooler?

2   Swab a little water onto the back of one hand with cotton wool and wave it backwards and forwards again.
    What does the wet part feel like compared with the dry parts?
    Note any feelings to do with temperature sense.

3   Dry your hand then swab a little alcohol onto it with cotton wool. Wave it backwards and forwards again.
    What does the alcohol-treated part feel like compared with the dry parts?
    Note any feelings to do with temperature sense.
    Does the alcohol give you a sensation which is different from water?

4   What conclusion can you draw at this stage of the experiment?

5   Obtain three thermometers. Record the temperature reading of each.
    Wrap the bulbs of all three thermometers in a thin layer of cotton wool. Tie it in place with cotton.
    Leave the thermometers to acclimatize for five minutes then record the temperature reading of each.

6   Take one thermometer (with dry cotton wool) and wave it backwards and forwards for one minute, then record the temperature reading.
    Take another thermometer, dip it into water, wave it backwards and forwards for one minute then record the temperature reading.

7   **Questions:**
    How do the results with a thermometer dipped in water and alcohol compare with those from the thermometer covered with dry cotton wool?
    How do the results of the thermometer experiment help explain the results from treating skin with water and alcohol?
    Alcohol evaporates more quickly than water. Use this information to explain results from both experiments.
    What do these results tell you about the function of perspiration?

More things to do

A chemist has invented a new, harmless liquid that evaporates quickly. He wants to sell it in swabs which people can use to wipe themselves when they are too hot.

Design an experiment to compare the effectiveness of this invention with a wet cloth.

The liquid and water must be compared under exactly the same conditions.
What control is necessary?

Food tests

You need:

iodine	liquid egg albumen
Benedict's reagent	bread
2% sodium hydroxide (Biuret A)	potatoes
1% copper sulphate (Biuret B)	cheese
ethanol	cooking oil
test tubes and racks	glucose
spotting tiles	starch powder
Bunsens, tripods and gauzes	milk powder
250 cm^3 beakers	peanuts
goggles	suet
glass rods	peas and beans
spatulas	carrots
bulb pipettes	grapes
sodium bicarbonate	

Begin by performing the following tests on known foods to observe a **positive result**. It is recommended that you then repeat each test with sodium bicarbonate to observe a **negative result**. These observations will be helpful when you go on to test foods of unknown composition.

1   **Test for starch**
    Place a little starch powder in a depression on a spotting tile.
    Add a few drops of iodine.
    Positive result: blue/black colour
    Negative result: brown colour

2   **Test for glucose**
    Place equal quantities of a strong glucose solution and
    Benedict's solution in a test tube (about 2 cm^3 of each).
    SAFETY: put on goggles.
    Lower the test tube into a beaker of boiling water, wait until
    the test tube contents boil and leave it for two minutes.
    Strong positive result: brick red precipitate
    Medium positive result: yellow orange precipitate
    Weak result: green colour
    Negative result: blue colour
    Before testing a solid food it must be crushed in warm water to
    extract any glucose which may be present.

3   **Test for proteins**
    Dissolve a little milk powder in water in a test tube. Add about
    2 cm³ of Biuret A solution. Add a few drops of Biuret B
    solution (do not boil).
    Positive result: purple colour
    Negative result: blue colour
    Note that this is a test for soluble proteins. Before testing a
    solid food it must be crushed in warm water to dissolve any
    proteins which may be present.

4   **Test for oil and fat**
    Place about 1 cm³ of ethanol in a test tube. Add a few drops of
    oil and mix by shaking. Add an equal amount of water and
    shake again.
    Positive result: a cloudy emulsion forms
    Negative result: liquid remains clear
    Food containing solid fats are tested by crushing them in
    ethanol to obtain an alcoholic solution. This is filtered and
    added to water.

More things to do

Use these tests to analyse the range of foods provided.
Divide each food into four samples and perform one test on each.
Remember to crush solid samples in warm water to extract glucose
and protein, and alcohol to extract fats and oils.
Make sure you know the difference between positive and
negative results.
Design a results table to show positive and negative results for
each test.
List the types of food found in each sample.

From your tests list the types of food present in bread, milk,
boiled potato and cheese.
Would eating these foods give you a balanced diet (i.e. do they
contain sufficient carbohydrate, protein and fat for health)?
What would be the result of basing your diet on these foods
alone?

> **Main skills assessed:**
>
> Follow instructions
> Use apparatus
> Record and handle data
> Draw conclusions
> Criticize an experiment

Measuring the energy value of foods

You need:

Bunsen burner	thermometers
wood splints	safety goggles
stands and clamps	measuring cylinder
boiling tubes	foods: peanuts, bacon,
mounted needles	sunflower seeds, bread

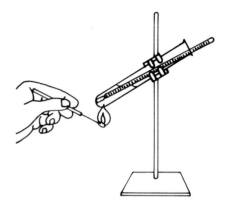

1 Put 20 cm³ of water into a boiling tube. Fix the tube in a clamp so that it is held at an angle of 45° (see diagram).

2 Weigh a peanut very carefully, in grams (if possible to two decimal places) and note the result.

3 Fix the peanut onto a mounted needle, taking care that no bits drop off.

4 Measure the temperature of the water in the boiling tube and note the result.

5 Ignite the peanut in a Bunsen flame. *Quickly* place the burning peanut under the boiling tube. The idea is to use as much heat as possible from the burning nut to heat the water in the tube.
If the nut goes out, relight it quickly and put it back under the tube.
When the peanut has completely burnt, measure the temperature of water in the boiling tube again and note the result.
When the peanut has completely burnt, measure the temperature of water in the boiling tube again and note the result.

6 Before you can go any further you must know:
• the mass (weight) of water in the boiling tube (1 cm³ of water weighs 1 g),
• the rise in temperature of water in the boiling tube,
• the mass (weight) of the peanut.

7 It takes 4.2 joules of energy to raise the temperature of 1 g of water by 1 °C, therefore you can calculate the energy given off by 1 g of peanut as follows:

$$\frac{\text{mass of water (in grams)} \times \text{rise in temperature} \times 4.2}{\text{mass of the peanut}}$$

8 Your result will be much lower than the actual energy value of 1 g of peanut. Give as many reasons as you can why this is so. Despite this fact, if you use this method to find out the energy value of other foods your results can still be compared. Why is this so?

More things to do

Use this method to find out the energy value (in joules per gram) of the foods provided, and any others you can think of. Produce a results table and compare the energy value of each food.

Design a method of measuring the energy value of powdery and liquid foods (e.g. sugar and cooking oil).

Design an improved method which will give a more accurate result. (**Hint**: is there a way of reducing heat loss to the air?)

Enzymes and digestion

<table>
<tr><td>

You need:

visking tubing

boiling tubes

test tubes

500 cm^3/250 cm^3 beakers

thermometers

wood splints

sticky labels

starch solution

diastase solution

Benedict's reagent

iodine solution

Bunsens, tripods and gauzes

spotting tiles

cotton thread

</td><td>

Main skills assessed:

Follow instructions
Form hypotheses/solve
  problems
Design and carry out
  experiments
Use apparatus
Record and handle data
Draw conclusions
Criticize an experiment

</td></tr>
</table>

1 Half fill a 500 cm^3 beaker with water and heat it to 37 °C. Keep it at this temperature by adding hot and cold water.

2 Label three boiling tubes A, B and C, fill them with water at 37 °C and put them in the beaker of water at this temperature.

3 Open three 15 cm lengths of visking tubing by rubbing them between your fingers under a running tap and tie one end of each securely with cotton.
Fill one length of visking tubing with starch solution, tie the open end with cotton, rinse it under a tap and place it in tube A.
Fill another length of visking tubing with diastase solution, tie the open end with cotton, rinse it under a tap and place it in tube B.
Fill the last length of visking tubing with equal amounts of well-mixed starch and diastase solutions, tie one end with cotton, rinse it under a tap and put it in tube C.
Make sure the visking tubing in each boiling tube is completely covered with water. Place all three in the 500 cm^3 beaker of water maintained at 37 °C.

4 Now test samples from the remaining solutions. Test the starch solution with iodine and Benedict's reagent (page 38). Test the diastase solution with iodine and Benedict's reagent.

5 After 10 minutes obtain water from around the visking tube in tubes A, B and C. Test each sample with iodine and Benedict's reagent.
Repeat after a further 10 minutes.
Devise a results table.

6 **Questions:**
What are iodine and Benedict's reagent used to test for?
Why were the starch and diastase solutions tested with iodine and Benedict's reagent?
What are tubes A and B for?
Does starch pass through visking tubing?
In this experiment what does pass through the visking tubing?
What do your results tell you about diastase, about visking tubing, and about the substance which passed through the visking tubing?
What part of the body does visking tubing represent?
Why are digestive enzymes necessary?

Find out: How temperature and pH affect enzymes

Design experiments to investigate the effects of temperature and pH on diastase.
Does it work best at body temperature and will it work above or below this temperature?
Find out if it works in acid or alkaline conditions in the body, and if it works at different pH levels.

Investigating the sense of touch

You need:

large corks	pins
ruler with millimetre graduations	plain paper

Which is the most sensitive area of your hand?
This experiment shows you how to find out.

1 Push two pins through a cork so that the pin heads are 3 mm apart (see diagram). Measure the gap very carefully with a ruler.

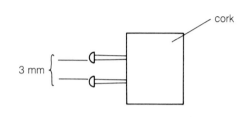

2 Put your hand palm downwards on a sheet of paper and trace round it with a pencil. Repeat, but this time with your palm upwards. Mark your drawings 'back' and 'palm'.

3 Work in pairs. One partner sits with eyes closed while the other does the experiment. Then you swap places.
 The idea is to touch your partner's skin lightly with the pin heads (*not* the points). Sometimes you touch with two heads and sometimes with one head – your partner *must not know* if it is two heads or one. Your partner must say, without looking, if one or two heads have been used.

4 Compare the areas of skin shown in the diagrams opposite:
 back of the hand   palm
 knuckles   front of fingers
 back of the fingers   finger tips

5 Starting with the back of the hand, touch your partner's skin with one or two heads until the skin has been touched a total of ten times.
 Only record your partner's answer *when you have used two heads* (i.e. ignore answers given when you touch with one head).
 If your partner says 'two' write a number 2 on the drawing of the hand in the area you are testing. If your partner says 'one' write a number 1 in this area.

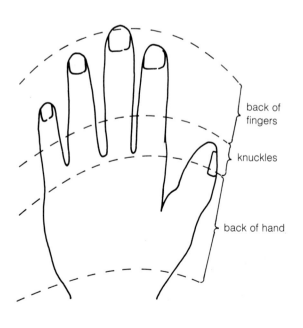

6 When you have ten results in one area move to the next.

7 **Understanding your results**
Look at each area in turn. If there are a lot of 2s in an area of
skin it is very sensitive, because your partner could tell the
difference between one head and two.
If there are a lot of 1s in an area it is not very sensitive because
your partner could not tell the difference between one head
and two.

8 **Make your results clearer**
Draw another pair of hand outlines, palm down and palm up.
Colour each area as follows:

nine to ten 2s   — *red*
seven to eight 2s   — *orange*
five to six 2s   — *yellow*
three to four 2s   — *green*
one to two 2s   — *light blue*
no 2s   — *dark blue*

9 **Questions:**
Which areas of hand are the most sensitive? List each area
from the most to the least sensitive.
Think of two reasons why some areas of skin are more
sensitive than others.
How is it possible for two pin heads to touch your skin but
you feel only one head?
What inaccuracies are there with this method?

10 Find out:
- how results are affected if you test each area with two
  corks: one with pin heads 1 cm apart and one with pin
  heads 3 mm apart,
- what happens if you test yourself using
  this method — are your results more or
  less accurate?

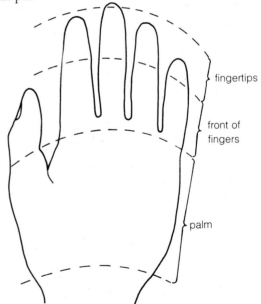

fingertips

front of
fingers

palm

Main skills assessed:

Follow instructions
Use apparatus
Record and handle data
Draw conclusions
Criticize an experiment

Investigating sensitivity to temperature

> **You need:**
>
> | | |
> |---|---|
> | 250 cm³ beakers | ice-cold water |
> | thermometers | hot water |
> | bulb pipettes | sticky labels |

Are some areas of your hand more sensitive than others to differences in temperature?

1 Label three beakers 25 °C, 35 °C and 45 °C. Use hot and ice-cold water to fill each beaker with water at these temperatures and keep them at this level during the experiment. Put a bulb pipette in each beaker.

2 The idea is to test the skin of one hand with water at different temperatures.
Work in pairs. One member sits facing away from the water samples, with a hand on the bench, while the other performs the tests.
Test:
    fingertips
    palm
    back of the fingers
    back of the hand.

3 Use a bulb pipette to place one drop of water carefully onto the area being tested. Your partner must say if it is hot, or warm or cold. Note the reply.
Test each area a total of 12 times, made up of four tests at each temperature. Choose different temperatures at random so that your partner does not know which to expect.

4 Design a suitable results table with correct and incorrect responses for each area recorded as ticks and crosses.

5 List the areas you tested from the most to the least sensitive. Explain your results.
Why is temperature sense useful?

Investigating sensory adaptation

6 Label three 250 cm³ beakers 'cold', 'warm' and 'hot'.
Fill the first with ice-cold water, the second with water at room temperature, and the third with hot (*not boiling*) water.

7 Place the beakers in a row with the water at room temperature in the middle.
Place the fingers of one hand in the hot water, and the fingers of the other hand in the cold water.
After one minute, place the fingers of both hands into the water at room temperature.

8 **Questions:**
Does the water feel different to each hand? Can you explain this result?
A traveller from the arctic and another from the tropics arrived in London on a warm Spring day. The traveller from the arctic thought that London's weather was warm, but the traveller from the tropics thought it was cold. Use your results to explain their feelings.
What does **sensory adaptation** mean?

> **Main skills assessed:**
>
> Follow instructions
> Use apparatus
> Record and handle data
> Draw conclusions
> Criticize an experiment

Investigating the sense of taste

You need:

50 cm³ beaker labelled 'sweet', containing sugar solution
50 cm³ beaker labelled 'salt', containing salt solution
50 cm³ beaker labelled 'sour', containing citric acid solution
50 cm³ beaker labelled 'bitter', containing bitter aloes

Your tongue has taste receptors, called **taste buds**. There are four kinds of taste bud: those which are sensitive to sweet, salt, sour and bitter tastes. This experiment shows you how to find out if the different kinds of taste bud are evenly spread over the tongue, or if certain areas have only one type.

Map of the tongue's taste areas

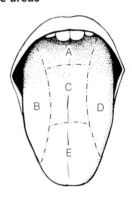

1   Copy the diagram of a tongue from the illustration opposite.

2   Work in pairs. One member of the pair, the subject, sits with eyes closed and his or her tongue sticking out.
    The other member, the experimenter, uses a bulb pipette to place *one drop* of liquid from a beaker onto the subject's tongue. The subject *must not know* which taste is being tested.
    The subject says which taste has been used.
    The experimenter notes the reply on a results table which should show:
       area of tongue tested
       taste tested
       correct/incorrect reply
       ease of reply (i.e. if the subject easily detected the taste or had difficulty and had to guess).

3   The mouth should be rinsed between tests. Each taste solution should be tested eight times — twice in every area shown on the diagram.

4   **Questions:**
    How do your results compare with the rest of the class?
    Do the areas marked on the diagram of the tongue correspond with one or more tastes?
    If there are only four different 'tastes', how are all the hundreds of different 'flavours' of food and drink produced?
    Why is taste necessary?

Main skills assessed:

Follow instructions
Use apparatus
Record and handle data
Draw conclusions
Criticize an experiment

Eyes and vision I

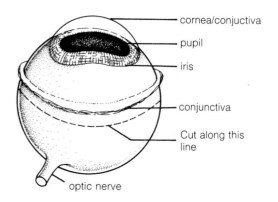

cornea/conjuctiva
pupil
iris
conjunctiva
Cut along this line
optic nerve

Eye dissection

1 Carefully remove any fat surrounding the eye.
   What are the muscles for, which are attached to the outside of the eyeball?
   Look for the **optic nerve** – it should look like a thick, yellow strand.

2 Using a sharp scalpel and/or scissors, cut through the tough, outer **sclerotic layer** somewhere on the line marked on the diagram opposite.
   Taking care not to squeeze the eye, continue cutting along this line until the eye can be separated into front and back halves.
   Lay the two portions in a dissecting tray of water so that the insides of front and back can be examined.

3 **Questions:**
   What is the jelly-like substance in the back of the eye?
   What is the colour of the inside surface of the eye? Why is it this colour?
   Find the point inside the back of the eye where the optic nerve leaves the eye. What is this point called?
   What are the black fibres which radiate outwards from the lens?
   Remove the lens and observe its shape. What happens to its shape when the eye is focused on near and distant objects?
   Look for the **iris** and **pupil**. What is the iris made of and what is its function?

Back of eye   **Front of eye**

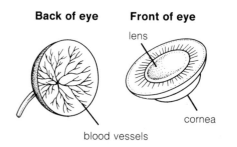

lens
cornea
blood vessels

Find your blind spot

4 Hold this book at arm's length. Close your left eye and stare at the cross below with your right eye. Note that, without looking directly at it, the black circle can still be seen. Bring the book slowly towards your face (*don't look away from the cross*). At a certain point the circle disappears. This happens when its image falls on the blind spot.

5 Why don't your blind spots stop you seeing properly?

Eyes and vision II

Distance judgement

This experiment shows you how to compare one eye with two eyes when judging distances. It should help you understand why we have two eyes.

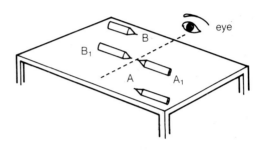

1 Arrange two pencils on a desk top in positions A and B, as shown on the diagram opposite.

2 Sit so that your eyes are level with the surface of the desk (it is very important that you do not look down on the desk).

3 The aim is to move the pencils until their points are exactly opposite but *not touching* (i.e. to positions A₁ and B₁). Do this in three different ways:
   Method one: Close one eye and ask a partner to move the pencils by *following your instructions only* (they must not try to correct your mistakes). Return the pencils to positions A and B.
   Method two: Close one eye but this time use *one hand* to move the pencils.
   Method three: Try the experiment again using one hand but *both eyes*.

4 **Questions:**
   Is there any difference between using one eye and two? If so try to explain this difference. What does this tell you about why we have two eyes?
   Is it easier or more difficult to use one hand or a partner to get the pencils opposite? If so try to explain any difference.

Three-dimensional vision

3-D vision allows you to see rounded, solid objects rather than a flat picture of your surroundings, like a photograph. This experiment helps you understand how your eyes and brain produce a 3-D vision.

5 Hold a large coin with its edge towards you, about 30 cm in front of your eyes.

6 Look at the coin first with your left eye closed and then with your right eye closed.

7 **Questions:**
   What is the difference between the two views of the coin?
   Why does your brain need these two views to produce a 3-D vision?
   Try to think of reasons why, despite these results, your vision does not become completely flat and two-dimensional when you close one eye. (Do we need two eyes after all?)

Balance and hearing

<table>
<tr><td>You need:

clear plastic tubing long enough to make a
ring 5 cm in diameter

whistle
blindfold</td><td>Main skills assessed:

Follow instructions
Record and handle data
Criticize an experiment</td></tr>
</table>

Investigating the organs of balance

1 Obtain a piece of wood or plastic which can be used to join the ends of the tube to make a watertight ring. Fill the tube with water but allow a small bubble of air to remain, then connect the tube ends.

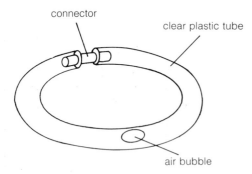

connector

clear plastic tube

air bubble

2 **Questions:**
What part of the inner ear does the tube represent?
Hold the tube horizontally, then tilt it from side to side. What happens to the bubble?
If the tube was lined with sensitive hairs, what would happen to them as the tube is tilted in this way?
How is this demonstration similar to what happens in your inner ear when you tilt your head from side to side?
Spin (**rotate**) the tube horizontally on a table top then stop it suddenly. What happens to the bubble?
What does this tell you about why people feel dizzy if they spin round and round and stop suddenly?

Why do we have two ears?

3 **Method one:** A blind-folded student sits in the centre of a classroom while another student, without shoes, moves *quietly* about the room making a noise, such as a clap, from different positions.
The blind-folded student tries to point in the direction of the claps.
Repeat the experiment while the blind-folded student covers one ear.

4 **Questions:**
Using two ears, is it more difficult to judge the direction of some claps than others? If so which direction do these claps come from?
Look at the shape of the ears. Does this help explain your results?
Are your results different when one ear is covered? If so, what does this tell you about why we have two ears?

5 **Method two:** A group of students line up on a playing field facing a teacher about 50 paces away.
• The students are blind-folded and try to find the teacher from memory.
• Blind-folded students try to find the teacher while he/she blows a whistle at one-second intervals.
• Blind-folded students with *one ear covered*, try to find the teacher while he/she blows a whistle.

6 **Questions:**
Compare your three results. What do they tell you about why we need two ears?
Using both ears, how do you know which direction a sound is coming from?
How will covering one ear upset direction-finding?

Reflexes

Main skills assessed:

Follow instructions
Record and handle data
Draw conclusions
Criticize an experiment

Measure the speed of your reflexes

1   Work in pairs. One student holds a ruler
    between thumb and forefinger so that the
    ruler hangs with its zero mark at the bottom.
    The other waits with thumb and forefinger of
    one hand about 2 cm apart and level with the
    zero mark of the ruler.

2   The student holding the ruler says 'ready',
    then drops the ruler within five seconds
    without further warning.
    The other student must catch the ruler
    between thumb and forefinger.
    Note the number of centimetres the ruler has
    dropped by looking a the position of the
    thumb and forefinger on the ruler.

3   Calculate the average distance over at least
    ten ruler drops. Use the graph opposite to
    convert this distance into response time, in
    seconds.
    Draw a graph showing the range of results
    for the whole class.

4   **Questions:**
    Name all the parts of the nervous system
    which impulses travel through as you
    respond to the ruler dropping.
    Your result is the time it takes for impulses to
    travel from your eyes to your hand. Measure
    this distance and use it to calculate the speed
    of nerve impulses, in metres per second.

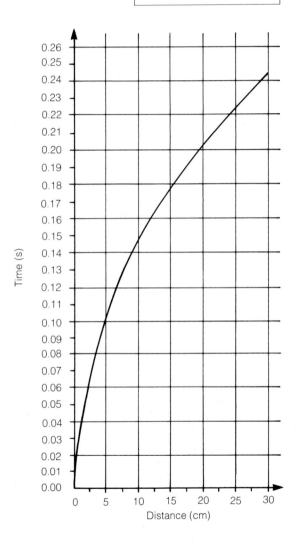

49

Investigating soil life

You need:

conical flasks	rubber and glass	Petri dishes of sterile
U-tubes	tubes	nutrient agar (p. 60)
taps or spring clips	soda lime	various soil samples
bungs with one hole	eosin or ink	incubator

Main skills assessed:

Follow instructions
Form hypotheses/solve
  problems
Design and carry out
  experiments
Use apparatus
Record and handle data
Criticize an experiment

Soil contains living things

1   Predict what will happen to liquid in the
    U-tube of the apparatus below when the taps
    are closed. (**Clue**: Living things take in
    oxygen and produce carbon dioxide at about
    the same rate. Carbon dioxide is absorbed by
    the soda lime.)

2   Prepare the apparatus, leave the taps open
    for at least five minutes, then close them and
    check your prediction.

3   **Questions:**
    Why does the coloured liquid move in the
    way you observed?
    What exactly is the apparatus measuring?
    Why was the sterilized soil included?

Find out: How inorganic fertilizers affect soil

Design an experiment, using this apparatus, to
find out if heavy doses of inorganic fertilizer and
various pesticides affect soil life. What factors
must remain the same? What controls are
needed? How will you treat soil samples?

Demonstrate the presence of microbes in soil

4   Sprinkle *a little* soil from a number of
    different sources into dishes of sterile
    nutrient agar. Label them and seal with
    sticky tape.

5   Incubate the dishes, upside down at about
    25 °C. Examine the dishes daily for growths
    of bacteria and fungi.

6   Compare the types of mould and bacterial
    colonies which appear from each soil sample
    (*Do not open the dishes. Observe the safety
    precautions on page 60.*)

Problem: Devise two controls for this
experiment to prove that the microbes come
only from soil and not from the air or
contaminated petri dishes.

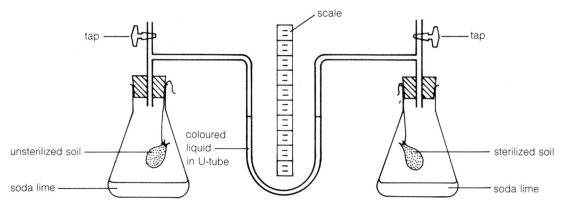

Investigate the functions of soil microbes

You need:

large plant pots   soil

safety goggles   large tin

graph paper   Bunsens and tripods

leaves from deciduous trees   distilled water

Main skills assessed:

Following instructions
Use apparatus
Record and handle data
Draw conclusions
Criticize an experiment

1   Obtain two leaves such as oak, beech or sycamore (not thick leathery leaves, like holly). Attach a piece of paper to their petioles and label them 'Leaf A' and 'Leaf B'. Weigh each leaf. Place each leaf on graph paper and carefully draw around it. Label the drawings 'Leaf A' and 'Leaf B'. Count the graph paper squares covered by the leaves to work out their area.
Write the area and weight of each leaf on the drawing.

2   Obtain enough rich loam soil to fill two large plant pots. Put half the soil in a tin.
Sterilize the soil by heating it over a Bunsen flame until it is completely burnt. *SAFETY: wear goggles.*

3   Label two large plant pots A and B.
Pot A: Half fill with soil, lay leaf A flat on the surface and pour in more soil until the pot is full. Water the soil with *distilled* water.
Pot B: Half fill with burnt soil, lay leaf B flat on the surface and pour in more burnt soil until the pot is full. Water with *distilled* water.

4   After two weeks empty the pots, keeping the soil separate and intact, to retrieve the leaves. Carefully wash off any soil and blot dry with paper towels, without damaging the leaves.

5   Compare the leaves visually. Reweigh them and compare with the original masses.
Draw their outlines on graph paper, marking any holes which have appeared. Label the drawings 'Leaf A (2 weeks)', and 'Leaf B (2 weeks)'.
Compare the area of each leaf with its original area.

6   Replant leaf A as before. Sterilize the soil from pot B again then replant leaf B as before.

7   Repeat steps **4**, **5** and **6** above at two-week intervals until there is a clear difference between the two leaves.

8   **Questions:**
What is the difference between the soils in pot A and pot B?
What changes occurred in the mass, and the area of each leaf?
What caused these changes?
How do these changes help maintain soil fertility?
'If it were not for the decay processes, demonstrated by this experiment, all plants and animals would die'. What is the reasoning behind this statement. Is it true?

How to compare soil samples

Use these tests to compare sandy, clay and loam soils, then construct a chart summarizing your results. These tests are especially useful when studying the relationship between soils and plant life in various habitats.

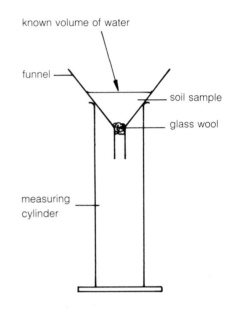

known volume of water

funnel

soil sample

glass wool

measuring cylinder

You need:

filter funnels	evaporating basins
glass wool	sand, clay and loam soils
stop-watch	crucibles
measuring cylinders	test tubes
tin cans	pipe-clay triangles
thermostatic oven	

Bunsen and tripods

soil samples from many different habitats

pH indicator chemicals (e.g. BDH indicators)

Investigating soil water

1   Water retention

Plug the neck of a filter funnel with a small wad of glass wool. Pour a known weight of dry, powdered soil into the filter funnel. Put the filter funnel on a measuring cylinder. Pour a known volume of water *gently* onto the soil and note the volume of water which eventually collects in the measuring cylinder. The difference between the two volumes is the amount of water retained by the soil.

2   Rate at which water percolates through soils

After completing experiment **1** above, start a stop-watch and at the same moment pour another known volume of water onto the wet soil. Note the time taken for this water to drain through the soil.

3   Water content of soil

Take a sample of wet soil after completing experiment **2** above (note that it contains as much water as the soil can hold onto against gravity).

Weigh the sample, place it in an evaporating basin. Heat it in a thermostatic oven at 100 °C for 30 minutes and weigh it again.

Repeat until no further loss in mass has occurred. The difference between the original mass and the mass after heating is the mass of water in the soil. Convert this to a percentage of the original mass.

4   Questions:

Compare the *volume* of water retained by a soil sample (experiment **1**) with the *mass* of water it contains (experiment **3**). Are both results the same? (1 cm^3 of pure water weighs 1g.)

How do sand clay and loam soil differ in their ability to retain water and allow water to percolate through?

Why is water retention and percolation different in sand, clay and loam?

Measuring the humus, mineral and air content of soils

5 Humus and mineral content of soils
Weigh a sample of the dry soil after completing experiment **3**.
Place the sample in a crucible and heat it strongly for about 20 minutes. *SAFETY: wear goggles.*
Weigh it again when cool.

6 Questions:
Why was the soil burnt?
How can you calculate the mass of humus and minerals in soil from your results?
Calculate the humus and mineral content of your soil as percentages.
In what ways does adding humus to a soil increase its fertility?

7 Air content of soil
Find the volume of an empty tin. Punch small holes in the bottom of the tin and push it, open end first, into the soil until its bottom is level with the soil surface.
Dig the tin out of the soil *without* disturbing its contents and remove soil until it is level with the open end of the tin.
Empty *all* the soil into a large measuring cylinder containing a known volume of water. After bubbles have stopped rising, note the water level.

8 Questions:
How can you calculate the air content of soil from your results?
Do sand, loam and clay contain different amounts of air. If so why?
Why is air an important part of soil?

Investigate soil particles and pH

Two very important features of soil are the amounts (**proportions**) of humus, silt, clay, sand and gravel that it contains and its pH. It is very easy to investigate these features with the following tests.

9 Soil particles
Half fill a measuring cylinder with soil, then fill to the top with water. Put your hand over the open end of the measuring cylinder and shake until soil and water are thoroughly mixed. Allow the soil to settle for at least five minutes.
Mineral particles settle in separate layers, the largest first. Humus floats to the top.
Use graduations on the measuring cylinder to estimate the proportions of each size of mineral particle in the soil, and the amount of humus.

10 Testing soil pH
Place a few drops of pH indicator on a white tile. Sprinkle a little soil into the indicator and mix thoroughly.
Tilt the tile so that the indicator runs out of the soil. Compare its colour with the chart provided with the indicator and read off its pH.

Find out:
- the names of some plants which grow best in acid, and in alkaline soil,
- some plants which can live in either acid or alkaline soils,
- which habitats are likely to have acid or alkaline soils (e.g. chalk grassland, moor, marsh, etc.).
- how you can change the pH of soil.

Main skills assessed:

Follow instructions
Use apparatus
Make measurements
Record and handle data
Draw conclusions
Criticize an experiment

Pollution

Main skills assessed:

Follow instructions
Form hypotheses/solve problems
Design and carry out experiments
Use apparatus
Make measurements
Record and handle data
Criticize an experiment

Air pollution − sticky tape method

The amount of dust, soot and other particles in the air can be investigated by exposing sticky tape to the atmosphere.

1 Fasten a length of transparent sticky tape, sticky side up, to a piece of white card. Leave it outside in dry weather for a day then examine it under a microscope. Can you see the difference between dust, soot, fibres and other types of dirt?

2 Calculate the area of the field of view: measure its diameter by focusing on the edge of a millimetre rule and divide this by two to find the radius. The formula $A=\pi r^2$ gives the area. How many particles are visible in this area?

Investigating air pollution

How many particles would there be in a square millimetre, and a square centimetre? Use this method to compare air pollution in a number of places from a city centre to open countryside. Can you pinpoint areas of heavy pollution where you live?
Investigate air pollution at various distances from the edge of a busy road.

Air pollution − leaf-wiping method

3 Find an evergreen shrub (privet, holly, etc.), dampen a white paper tissue and use it to wipe a leaf.
Try new leaves and old leaves. Can you see

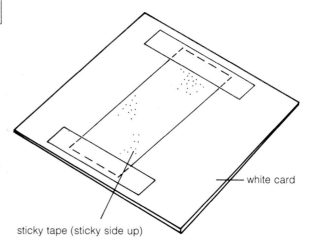

white card

sticky tape (sticky side up)

any difference in the black marks on the paper?
Why use evergreen shrubs?

Find out: About dirt on leaves

Measure the amount of dirt on a shrub's leaves in grams per square metre.

Use the leaf-wiping method to solve this problem then compare the amount of dirt on shrubs from a city centre outwards.
Start by thinking about the following:
Decide how many leaves you should wipe on each shrub.
How will you weigh the amount of dirt on its leaves?
How could you use graph paper to estimate the area of a leaf?
What would be the best time of year to do this investigation?
Why is it only a very rough estimate of air pollution?

Acid rain

4   Collect rain as it falls in clean glass jars.

5   Test the water with universal pH test papers to measure its acidity. (Note that pure rain has a pH of 5.7 because it absorbs carbon dioxide from the air to become carbonic acid.) With dry fingers, tear out one leaf from a book of test papers. Dip the paper into the water and quickly put in on a white tile. Compare its colour with the chart provided with the test papers.

Water pollution

The cleanliness of a stream or pond can often be judged by studying 'indicator animals' known to tolerate different amounts of water pollution. Use the chart below and the drawings to grade streams and ponds into categories from A (clean) to E (completely dead).

6   **Questions:**
Does city centre rain have a different pH from countryside rain?
Is there a difference in pH between day-time and night-time rain?
Are streams and ponds in your area acidified? (Fresh water should have a pH of about 6.5.)

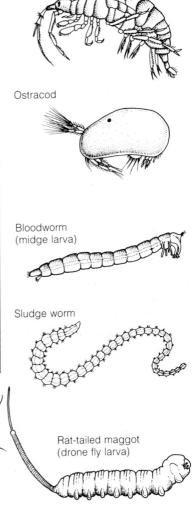

Freshwater shrimp

Ostracod

Bloodworm (midge larva)

Sludge worm

indicator animals	pollution category	pollution status
no apparent life	E	heavily polluted
sludge worms rat-tailed maggots	D	serious pollution
animals from D plus: ostracods blood worms	C	fairly serious pollution
animals from C and D plus: caddisfly larvae freshwater shrimps	B	some pollution
animals from B to D plus: stonefly nymphs mayfly nymphs	A	clean

Mayfly larva

Stonefly larva

Caddisfly larva

Rat-tailed maggot (drone fly larva)

Ecology I

<table>
<tr><td>

You need:

string
poles (3 metres long)
metre rules
spirit level

notebooks
graph paper
plant identification books
tent pegs

</td><td>

Main skills assessed:

Follow instructions
Form hypotheses/solve problems
Design and carry out experiments
Use apparatus
Record and handle data
Draw conclusions
Criticize an experiment

</td></tr>
</table>

Making a line transect

Many habitats have areas where vegetation and animal life changes from one type to another, such as down a hillside or the banks of a stream. These changes can be studied by making a **line transect**. This is a record of the types of plant (and certain animals) which live on a line across a habitat.

1 Mark a length of string at 1 m or smaller intervals and stretch it between two pegs across the habitat so that it crosses an area of change.

2 On sloping ground another string can be stretched across the same line between two poles and arranged above the ground so that it is horizontal. At regular intervals along the slope measure the distance between the string and the ground. Use this information to draw an outline of the slope on graph paper.

3 Starting at one end of the transect, record the plants which touch the first string at certain intervals (e.g. 10, 50, or 100 cm depending on the density of the vegetation).

4 Using symbols to represent each species, record the plants along the transect on graph paper (see example below).

Projects

5 Study the changes:
- down the banks of a stream or pond,
- from the upper sea shore down to low tide level on rocky and other shorelines (show attached animals such as barnacles, limpets, mussels etc.),
- from a shaded to an unshaded area,
- across a path to study the effects of trampling on vegetation,
- up an overgrown wall from ground level.

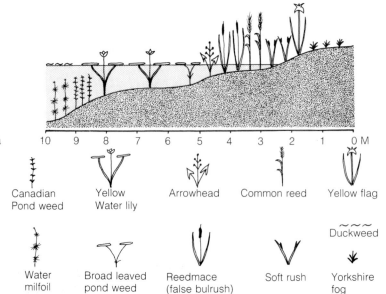

Canadian Pond weed — Yellow Water lily — Arrowhead — Common reed — Yellow flag

Water milfoil — Broad leaved pond weed — Reedmace (false bulrush) — Soft rush — Duckweed — Yorkshire fog

6 Look carefully at the plants (and animals) along your transect and try to work out *why* there is a change from one type to another.
Does the soil pH level change?
Does the soil water content change?
Does the type of soil change (e.g. from clay to sand)?
Does one area get more light than another?
Is one area more exposed to wind than the other?

7 Look for adaptations to these and other changing conditions across a habitat.
How are the plants adapted to live in wet or dry conditions, or windy or sheltered conditions, or shaded or unshaded conditions etc.?
Does animal life change as the vegetation changes? If so, in what ways?

Making a belt transect

This is a record of vegetation in a narrow strip, or belt, across a habitat. It is useful where a line transect fails to show enough plants to make a worthwhile record.

8 Peg out two parallel lines 1 metre apart and as long as you wish across a habitat. Study the area one square metre at a time by dividing it into 1 metre squares with string.

9 Choose symbols to represent one plant which grows in patches, or patches of several different plants which grow together (see example below).

10 Record your results by drawing the area to scale on graph paper.

Projects

11 A belt transect can be constructed instead of a line transect in each of the projects mentioned opposite.

12 Colonization
Belt transects can be used to study **colonization**, which is the appearance of plants and animals in a cleared area of a habitat. Peg out two parallel lines 1 metre apart and 3 metres long on grassland. Dig out all vegetation from the central square metre, removing as many roots as you can but leaving as much soil as possible.
Record vegetation in the undisturbed part of the belt and, at monthly intervals, record plants growing in the cleared area. What do your results tell you about how one set of plants gives way to another in **ecological succession**.

13 Devise a method of studying the colonization of rock on a sea shore by sea weeds and animals.

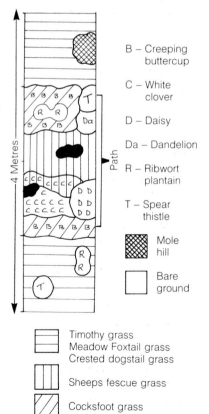

B – Creeping buttercup

C – White clover

D – Daisy

Da – Dandelion

R – Ribwort plantain

T – Spear thistle

Mole hill

Bare ground

Timothy grass
Meadow Foxtail grass
Crested dogstail grass

Sheeps fescue grass

Cocksfoot grass

A belt transect across a grassland path showing the effects of trampling

Ecology II

You need:

25 cm quadrats	notebooks
graph paper	identification books
enamel paint	(plant and animal)
paint solvent	white pie dishes
fine paint brush	specimen tubes

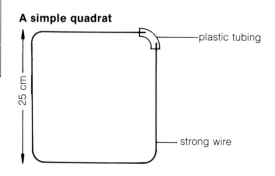

A simple quadrat

plastic tubing

25 cm

strong wire

Random sampling of plant life

How would you answer the question, 'Which types of plant are the most common in this habitat?' You could count all the different types of plant but this is not necessary except for very small habitats. An easier method is called **random sampling**. To do this you use a square or rectangular frame called a **quadrat** to study several small areas (**samples**) of the habitat chosen at random.

You place a quadrat at random throughout a habitat by throwing one over your shoulder. Do not deliberately throw it to land on vegetation which looks interesting. What you do next depends on the information you require. This could be the *density, frequency* or *percentage cover* of various types of plant.

1 **Density** This is the number of plants (or animals) in a unit area of habitat (e.g. the number per 25 centimetre square). To discover the density of a plant species in a habitat, you count the number of this species present inside the area of a quadrat each time it lands. Continue until the quadrat has been cast throughout the whole habitat, then calculate the average number of times the species was found.

2 **Frequency** This is the number of times that a particular species is found when a quadrat is thrown a certain number of times. To calculate frequency you count the number of different species within the quadrat each time it lands and note their names. If, for example, you throw it a hundred times you note the number of times each species was found and express each result out of a hundred. This will tell you the most common (most frequent) species in the habitat, then the next most common, down to the rarest.

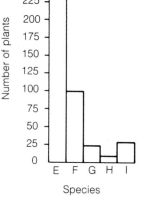

Histogram 1: lightly trampled region

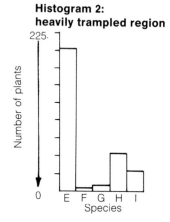

Histogram 2: heavily trampled region

3 **Percentage cover** This is the percentage of the total area of a habitat which each species covers. This can only be calculated with species which grow in clumps or large patches. Estimate the percentage cover of the species found inside a quadrat each time it lands, then calculate the average cover over a number of throws.

Project

You can use these methods to compare different habitats.

4 Study the boundary between one habitat and the next to discover how plant frequencies change.
Make lists of plants from the most frequent to the rarest in each habitat.
Where possible find the percentage cover of the commonest plants in each habitat.
Present results as histograms.

Studying animal populations

One aim of studying animal populations is to list species from the most common to the rarest. This is difficult because animals move in and out of an area, but there are ways of solving this problem.

5 **Comparative method** Carefully search the habitat and compare the numbers of each species you find. Give each species a score: five for the most frequently met and one for the rarest. If several groups work independently, average scores can be obtained.

6 **Capture-recapture method** You can estimate the total population of species which can be caught easily and marked in some way, and which disperse quickly when released, e.g. dragonflies, large beetles, snails, crabs, woodlice, water boatmen, etc.
Catch a number of specimens, mark them with brightly coloured enamel paint or liquid paper then release them.
After a day or two, when they have thoroughly dispersed, try to capture the same number again.
Note the number of marked specimens in the second catch.
An estimate of the total population of this species is calculated by this formula:

$$\text{Population} = \frac{\text{total in first catch x total in second catch}}{\text{number of marked specimens in second catch}}$$

Question 1

The histograms on the opposite page show the number of plants found in random samples taken in lightly trampled and heavily trampled grassland.
Which species is most affected by trampling?
Which species is least affected?
Study trampled areas and try to find out which plants can live there.
Try to explain how some plants are adapted to withstand trampling.
Explain how you would obtain random samples like these.

Question 2

Some students caught 50 crabs in a 25 m² area of sea shore, marked them with yellow paint then released them. Four days later they caught another 50 crabs. Thirteen of these were marked with yellow paint.
What is the estimated total crab population for this area?
Why is this only a rough estimate of the crab population?

Main skills assessed:

Follow instructions
Use apparatus
Record and handle data
Draw conclusions
Criticize an experiment

Microbiology: safety precautions and techniques

Safety precautions in microbiology

Microbiology practicals involve growing live bacteria and moulds. Observe these precautions to avoid health risks.

- Wash your hands after an experiment.
- Cover any cuts with waterproof dressing before handling cultures.
- Don't put anything in your mouth during an experiment.
- Seal lids of apparatus containing live bacteria with sticky tape. *Do not open them* to look at the bacteria.
- If a culture is spilled, flood the area with strong disinfectant and call a teacher.
- Destroy cultures *without opening them* by heating in a pressure cooker for 15 minutes. Containers can then be opened and washed.

Basic techniques

- Sterilize apparatus in a pressure cooker for 15 minutes before use, so you can be certain that bacterial growths come from a chosen source and *not* from dirty apparatus.

- Bacteria can be grown in tubes of **nutrient broth**: 1 g beef extract, 1 g peptone, 0.2 g yeast extract, 0.5 g sodium chloride dissolved in every 100 cm³ of nutrient broth. Sterilize before use.

- Bacteria can be grown in Petri dishes of **nutrient agar jelly:** 1.5 g of agar powder dissolved in every 100 cm³ of nutrient broth. Sterilize before use.

- Wire loops are used to transfer living bacteria from one container to another. First dip the loop in alcohol, then pass it through a flame to sterilize it. Innoculate agar plates as follows:
  a) Dip a sterilized loop into a bacterial culture.
  b) Open the lid of a petri dish just enough to let you wipe the surface of the agar with the loop.
  c) Close the lid, seal it with sticky tape and put it, upside down, in an incubator.
  Use harmless bacteria, e.g. *Escherichia coli* from a reputable supplier.

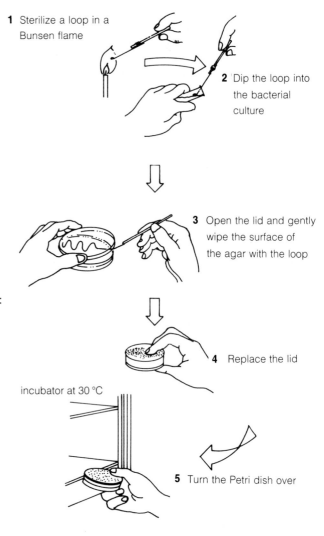

1 Sterilize a loop in a Bunsen flame

2 Dip the loop into the bacterial culture

3 Open the lid and gently wipe the surface of the agar with the loop

4 Replace the lid

incubator at 30 °C

5 Turn the Petri dish over

Growing and studying bacteria

You need:

Petri dishes of sterile
   nutrient agar and tubes
   of nutrient broth (p. 60)
bacteria culture

incubator
various disinfectants
sterile bulb pipettes

Bacteria are all around us

1 Label five sterile Petri dishes of nutrient agar A to E.

2 **Dish A:** Take off the lid and expose the agar to air in the laboratory for a hour. Replace the lid and seal it with sticky tape.
Dish B: Sprinkle a little dust from a bench surface or the floor onto the surface of the agar, replace the lid and seal it.
Dish C: Add a few drops of rain water to the agar, replace the lid and seal it.
Dish D: Add a dead fly. Replace the lid and seal it.
Dish E: Add a few drops of distilled water, replace the lid and seal it.

3 *SAFETY: never culture material from a lavatory, sewage-polluted water or an animal cage.*

4 Incubate the Petri dishes upside down for at least 48 hours at 15 °C to 30 °C.

5 Count the number of bacteria and mould colonies on each plate.
What is the function of dish E?
What conclusions can you draw from these results?

Investigate the effects of disinfectant on bacteria

6 Prepare five test tubes of sterile nutrient broth and label them A to E.
Add three drops of bacteria culture to each tube and replace the cotton wool plug.

7 **Tube A:** Add 5 cm³ of full strength disinfectant, replace the plug and seal it with sticky tape.
Tube B: 5 cm³ of disinfectant diluted to $\frac{1}{10}$ of full strength, replace the plug and seal it.
Tube C: Add 5 cm³ of disinfectant diluted to $\frac{1}{100}$ of its full strength, replace the plug and seal it.
Tube D: Add 5 cm³ of disinfectant diluted to $\frac{1}{1000}$ of its full strength, replace the plug and seal it.
Tube E: Add 5 cm³ of distilled water, replace the plug and seal it.

8 Incubate the tubes at 25 °C to 30 °C for at least 48 hours. Compare the cloudiness (**turbidity**) of each.
What conclusions can you draw about the effect of disinfectant on bacterial growth?

More things to do

Design experiments, using harmless bacteria, to compare the effects of other disinfectants, antiseptics and household bleach on bacterial growth.
Is one product more powerful than the others?

The effects of temperature on bacteria

You need:

sterilized test tubes	nutrient broth (p. 60)
plugged with sterile	bacterial culture
cotton wool	refrigerator
Bunsen, tripod and gauze	wire loops
incubator	500 cm³ beakers

Main skills assessed:

Follow instructions
Form hypotheses/solve problems
Design and carry out experiments
Use apparatus
Record and handle data
Criticize an experiment

Investigate the effects of cold and warm temperatures on bacteria

1　Add a few drops of bacteria culture to a bottle of nutrient broth.
Pour 2 cm³ of the broth into each of three sterilized test tubes, plug each with sterile cotton wool and label the tubes A, B and C.

2　Incubate the tubes as follows:
Tube A at 4 °C (the average temperature of a domestic refrigerator)
Tube B at room temperature
Tube C at about 60 °C

3　Observe the tubes daily for signs of cloudiness (**bacterial growth**).

4　What conclusions can you draw from your results about the effects of temperature on the growth of bacteria?

Investigate the effects of high temperatures on bacteria

5　Pour 2 cm³ of nutrient broth into each of six sterile test tubes, add a few drops of bacterial culture then plug them with sterile cotton wool.
Leave the tubes in a warm place for a day.

6　Call the next day 'day one'.
Day one:　Boil all six tubes in a beaker of water for five minutes then put them in a warm place.
Day two:　Put two tubes on one side in a warm place and label them A and B. Boil the other four tubes for five minutes and put them in a warm place.

Day three:　Put two tubes on one side in a warm place and label them C and D. Boil the other two for five minutes then label them E and F. Put them with the others in a warm place.

7　**Questions:**
How many times have each pair of tubes been boiled?
What effect does this have on the growth of bacteria inside them?
Boiling kills bacteria but not their reproductive spores. How does this explain your results?

8　**Find out** if results are different when this method is repeated but this time the tubes are placed in a pressure cooker for five minutes instead of boiling.
What is the difference between pressure cooking and boiling?
Does this affect bacterial spores?

Find out:　How well a refrigerator works

Design an experiment to find out how long it is safe to keep food in a domestic refrigerator:
- if the food is kept in the refrigerator all the time,
- if the food is taken out for half an hour each day then put back again (as could happen, for example, with cooked meat).

How will you check food for the presence of bacteria? Visible checking is not good enough.

The effects of soap and pH on bacteria

<table>
<tr><td>

You need:

Petri dishes of sterile
   nutrient agar and tubes
   of nutrient broth (p. 60)
bacteria culture

warm water for hand washing
soap and paper towels
incubator
sterile bulb pipettes

</td><td>

Main skills assessed:

Follow instructions
Form hypotheses/solve
   problems
Design and carry out
   experiments
Use apparatus
Record and handle data
Criticize an experiment

</td></tr>
</table>

How clean are your hands?

1 Label four Petri dishes of sterile nutrient agar A, B, C and D.

2 **Dish A:** Take off the lid for 10 seconds then replace it and seal around the rim with sticky tape.
Dish B: Take off the lid and press the fingers of an *unwashed* hand onto the agar (it must not be broken up by too much pressure). Replace the lid within 10 seconds and seal it.
Dish C: Wash your hands in warm water only (no soap). Dry them with paper towels. Take off the lid and touch the agar as before. Replace the lid within 10 seconds and seal it.
Dish D: Wash your hands *thoroughly* using warm water and soap. Dry them with paper towels. Take off the lid, touch the agar as before, replace the lid within 10 seconds and seal it.

3 Incubate the petri dishes upside down at 37°C for a week. *Without opening them:*
  a) count the number of bacteria colonies in each dish,
  b) count the number of different colonies in each dish,
  c) design a results table.
What do your results tell you about the cleanliness of washed and unwashed hands and the effectiveness of soap as a cleaning agent?

More things to do

A hospital wishes to test a new bactericidal soap for cleaning the hands of surgeons. Design an experiment to compare the new soap with the one they already use.

How clean are plates, cutlery, kitchen work surfaces, etc. after you have washed them? Design an experiment to answer this question.

Investigate the effects of pH on bacterial growth

4 Add 8 cm³ of sterile nutrient broth to each of five sterile boiling tubes.

5 Add 1 cm³ of 0.1M hydrochloric acid to tube A.
Add 1 cm³ of 0.0001M hydrochloric acid to tube B.
Add 1 cm³ of distilled water to tube C.
Add 1 cm³ of 0.0001M sodium hydroxide to tube D.
Add 1 cm³ of 0.1M sodium hydroxide to tube E.

6 Innoculate each tube with 1 cm³ of bacterial culture, plug them with cotton wool and seal with sticky tape.
Incubate the tubes at 25 °C to 30 °C for 48 hours.
Compare the cloudiness (turbidity) of each tube. What do your results tell you about the effect of pH on bacterial growth?

More things to do

Onions and other vegetables can be preserved in weak acids such as vinegar. Design an experiment to find out the strength of vinegar needed to preserve vegetables at room temperature for at least a month.

Index